TABLE OF CONTENTS

INTERVIEW

ANGELA CONSOLO MANKIEWICZ POETRY PRIZE

THIS YEAR'S JUDGE: B.J. BUCKLEY

INTERVIEW

POETRY II

TABLE OF CONTENTS

ESSAYS & MICRO-FICTION

CONTRIBUTORS

#9 Num.9 Number Nine, #9 Num.9 Number Nine, #9 Num.9 Number Nine, #9
 No.9 Number Nine, #9 Num.9 Number Nine, #9 Num.9 Number Nine, #9
Num.9 Number Nine, #9 Num.9 Number Nine, #9 Num.9 Number Nine, #9
No.9 Number Nine, #9 Num.9 Number Nine, #9 Num.9 Number Nine, #9
Num.9 Number Nine, #9 Num.9 Number Nine, #9 Num.9 Number Nine, No.9
Number Nine, #9 Num.9 Number Nine, #9 Num.9 Number Nine, #9, #9, No.
9 Number Nine, #9 Num.9 Number Nine, #9 Num.9 Number Nine, #9, No.9
No. Nine, #9 Num.9 Number Nine, #9 Num.9 Number Nine, #9, No.9
Number Nine, #9 Num.9 Number Nine, #9 Num.9 Number Nine, #9 No.9
No.Nine, #9 Num.9 Number Nine, #9 Num.9 Number Nine, #9, No.9 Number
Nine, #9 Num.9 Number Nine, #9 Num.9 Number Nine, #9, No.9 No. Nine,
 #9 Num.9 Number Nine, #9 Num.9 Number Nine, #9, No.9 Number Nine,
#9 Num.9 Number Nine, #9 Num.9 Number Nine, #9, No.9 Number Nine, #9
 Num.9 Number Nine, #9 Num.9 Number Nine, #9, No.9 Number Nine, #9
Num.9 Number Nine, #9 Num.9 Number Nine, #9, No.9 Number 9, #9 No.
9 Number Nine, #9 Num.9 Number Nine, #9, No.9 Number Nine, #9 Num.9
Number Nine, #9 Num.9 Number Nine, #9, No.9 Number Nine,#9 Num.9 No.
Nine, #9 Num.9 Number Nine, #9, Num.9 Number Nine, #9 Num.9 Number
Nine, #9 Num.9 Number Nine, Num.9 Number Nine, #9 Num.9 Number Nine,
No.9, Num.9 Number Nine, #9 Num.9 Number Nine, #9 Num.9 Number Nine,
#9 Num.9 Number Nine, #9 Num.9 #Nine, #9 Num.9 Number Nine, #9 Num.9
Number Nine, #9 Num.9 Number Nine, #9 Num.9 Number Nine,   #9 Num.9
No.9, Num.9 Number Nine, #9 Num.9 Number Nine, #9 Num.9 Number Nine,
Number Nine, #9 Num.9 Number Nine, #9 Num.9, Number Nine, #9 Num.9
No.9, Num.9 Number Nine, #9 Num.9 Number Nine, #9 Num.9 Number Nine,
Number Nine, #9 Num.9 Number Nine, #9 Num.9, No.9, Num.9 Number Nine
#9 Num.9 Number Nine, #9 Num.9 Number Nine, #9, Number Nine, #9 No.
9 Number Nine, #9 Num.9 Number Nine, #9 Num.9 No.9, Number Nine, #9;
<cue the weird music>
#9 Num.9 Number Nine, #9 Num.9 Number Nine, #9 Num.9 Number Nine,
No.9, Num.9 Number Nine, #9 Num.9 Number Nine, #9 Num.9 Number Nine,
#9 Num.9 Number Nine, #9 Num.9 Number Nine, #9 Num.9 Number Nine,
No.9, Num.9 Number Nine, #9 Num.9 Number Nine, #9 Num.9 Number Nine,
#9 Num.9 Number Nine, #9 Num.9 Number Nine, #9 Num.9 Number Nine,
No.9, Num.9 Number Nine, #9 Num.9 Number Nine, #9 Num.9 Number Nine,
#9 Num.9 Number Nine, #9 Num.9 Number Nine, #9 Num.9 Number Nine,
<I'm serious now! Cue the weird music!>
No.9, Num.9 Number Nine, #9 Num.9 Number Nine, #9 Num.9 Number Nine,
No.9, Num.9 Number Nine, #9 Num.9 Number Nine, #9 Num.9 Number Nine,
#9, #9, #9, #9, #9, #9, #9, #9, #9, #9, #9, #9, #9, #9, #9, #9,
No.9, Num.9 Number Nine, #9 Num.9 Number Nine, #9 Num.9 Number Nine,
#9, #9, #9, #9, #9, #9, #9, #9, #9, #9, #9, #9, #9, #9, #9, #9,
No.9, Num.9 Number Nine, #9 Num.9 Number Nine, #9 Num.9 Number Nine,
#9, #9, #9, #9, #9, #9, #9, #9, #9, #9, #9, #9, #9, #9, #9, #9,

THE VIEW FROM DOWN HERE

by RD Armstrong

FIRST, I have to thank my many patrons, some of whom have stuck by me for over twenty years! They are: **Georgia Cox, Dr. Brod, Chris Courter, Heath Ledger, Lawrence Welsh, Mike West, Frank Kearns, Carter Monroe, D.A. Pratt, Eric Paul Shaffer, Bill Mohr, Bill Gainer, Richard Grove** and **Patrick Conners**.

Second, a BIG shout out (or whatever the kids are saying these days) to all the poets and artists who submitted to this year's Anthology and poetry contest. For the list of participants, see the back cover. The number of participants has been declining over the last few years, hence my belief that it's time to move on to another format. *Next year*, I hope to put out an **E-zine**, hosted on **ISSUU**.

Third, as of 2021, I will be moving my support of the poetic community to a more hands-on approach. I'm working on an outfit that will offer Grants to poets in need, and to Poetry Centers, Food Banks, homeless shelters and Covid units in hospitals. The Scholarships will go to students who show promise, poetry-wise. I think Beyond Baroque and Libros Schmibros are interested in the Scholarships program at the **Moon in the Bucket Fund**, which is handling this new phase (see **In Haiku** - 3rd poem in the poetry section for the origin). Beyond Baroque will act as Fiscal Receiver for this little project until I can get my bearings. At this point, it's a one dog operation.

MOON IN THE BUCKET EXPLANATION

I think the image of the *Moon In The Bucket* represents a *safe place* to hold one's hopes and dreams... The idea that there's always the moon in the bucket, come rain or snow, is somehow reassuring; something you can rely on (lord knows, we all need something certain in this crazy world).

How'd this happen? About 10 years ago, when the money wasn't coming in as fast as I needed, I turned to an outfit up in Santa Barbara, I think Paul Fericano was involved with them (can't remember the name of the group). Their purpose was to help poets experiencing financial difficulty. Within a week they sent me a check, which really helped! But this type of help is no longer available, which I think is a shame. So, I'm stepping up to fill the gap.

The Martha F. Armstrong Scholarship Fund (named after my mother) will help meet the need to keep talented young poets on track. I'm also looking to offer support to poetry organizations around the country, like Woodland Pattern Book Center (Milwaukee, WI) one of the first organizations that I donated to; Libros Schmibros (East L.A.) and Teatro Paraguas (Santa Fe, NM). This is where I do my New Mexico Readings (tho I guess I'll be organizing ZOOM readings for this year and the next).

THE LAST HURRAH

Since LUMMOX Press put out its first publication back in 1994, I've published over 200 titles (mostly by other poets). It's kind of mind-blowing when you think about it! During the past 26 years, I put out a monthly Lit/Arts mag/zine (the LUMMOX Journal); I also put out a chapbook series called the **Little Red Books**. Since then I've been publishing perfect bound books, including 7 or 8 of my own.

But I found myself missing the hubbub of putting out a big anthology, so in 2011 I started a series called LUMMOX. I had planned on running this series for 10 issues (yearly), but sadly, it looks like **NINE** will be the *last* print version. I just can't do this anymore. My CRS has made it too hard and I can't keep my focus, can't keep up with the necessary steps to juggle all the parts to do this book (let alone doing 2 books simultaneously.... what was I thinking)! BTW the other book is called **Last Call, Chinaski!** It's an anthology too, full of poetry, stories, essays and illustrations from 85 fans. Why now you ask? It's Buk's centennial year, his birthday is August 16th!

So, it's with a heavy heart that I tell you that I'll be stepping away from my duties at LUMMOX Press for awhile. As a result of my own "numbing down", I won't be taking on any *new* book projects next year, but I'll still be self-publishing and doing the occasional special book project (I also have a few books I agreed to do, which will be published in 2021). LUMMOX Press isn't going away just yet.

But I have to tell you that dedicating my life (well a quarter century) to serving poets and poetry has not been as rewarding, especially over the last 5 years, as I had hoped. In late July, I started the Moon in the Bucket Fund, giving out over $6,000 thus far! Man I gotta say that I haven't been this happy in a long, long time!

Even so, I've got to thank all the poets that have sent me their poetry over the past 25 years... there must be at least 2,000! *THANK YOU ALL AND I WISH YOU ALL THE BEST!!!*

I've needed a break like this, I might even go camping! One thing for sure, I'll be doing some traveling.

I'm looking forward to traveling around the US, pressing the flesh (or whatever body part is considered safe) with my many poetry friends, here and in Canada and generally seeing the USA for the first time...in my Lummox-mobile, my pop-up book & gift shop. After spending most of my life in a self-imposed poverty, I suddenly find myself with enough funds to finance a 'happy' lifestyle (something I thought I'd never see). *Whoopie!!!*

IN THIS ISSUE

Poets in LUMMOX #9 hail from the U.S. (22 states), Canada, the U.K. (England, Ireland and Wales), Tunisia, India and Australia.

Apart from the usual avalanche of *high-quality poetry* and *creative writing*, there are two (2) interviews in this issue! I interviewed **Basia Miller**, a talented poetess from Santa Fe, NM and in the second, **Coco** interviews **Don Kingfisher Campbell,** the Poet King of Pasadena. There are clearly 2 different styles of interviewing here. Also the winners of the **Angela Consolo Mankiewicz Poetry Prize** (*which will continue next year,* btw) are featured; they are **John B. Lee** (Port Dover, ON, CAN.) – first prize; **Elaine Mintzer** (Manhattan Beach, CA) – second prize; **Alexis Fancher** (San Pedro, CA) – third prize; **Frank Kearns** (Downey, CA) and **Henry Crawford** (Silver Springs, MD) – Honorable Mentions.

I must thank **B.J. Buckley** for doing a stellar job judging the Contest! Here's what **B.J.** Said about this year's crop: *"The work submitted to this contest was a truly amazing group of poems. I've judged a number of such competitions over the years, and most times only a few truly shine out. Not so here; the variety of form and subject matter, as well as the attention to voice and craft by every single author made it very very difficult to winnow."* See if you agree with her.

There are a number of essays, articles and micro-fictions for your "dancing and dining pleasure": Part 2 of Charlie Plymell's **Eating With The Beats** (set in late 60s San Francisco); April Bulmer gives us **The Healer**; Coco's article on **The Making of the Common Book**, gives an interesting perspective on a community workshop that teaches how to create a book; Joe Farley's story, **At The Station**, shows that he's a multi-talented writer; new-comer Jesse James Kennedy's prose piece, **The Suburbs**, gives the reader a bit of stream-of-conscious writing; Marie C. Lecrivain's story, **What if Maria Gorreti Wanted Access to Birth Control?**, is thought provoking; longtime friend/patron of LUMMOX, Mike Meloan's microfiction **Mr. Jeeter** is another one of his quirky "slice of life" pieces; John Macker profiles Colorado poet **Tony Moffeit's "Rattlesnake Mojo"**; new member of the LUMMOX family, Mike Mahoney, attempts to make sense out of language in **33 Ways to "Make Common Words Uncommon Again"** (an idea put forth by Lawrence Ferlinghetti); Linda Singer's prose piece, **A Masked Woman Goes for a Walk** – life during Covid, right? Rick Smith, the harmonica tooting, word-slinging LUMMOX alumnus, details the time he and his parents were **Snowed in With Carl Sandburg** (American Poet – 1878-1967). Nancy Shiffrin (last year's ACM Contest Winner) reviews **The Collected Poems of Sylvia Plath.**

People often ask me why I don't have themes for the various iterations of the annual LUMMOX, and I tell them that a "theme" develops organically in every issue (even the ones that have a theme). This is issue is no different. Apart from the obvious 600 pound covid spore floating in the corner, waiting to insert itself into the international conversation (**PUT ON YER DAMN MASK!!**), there's definitely a Covid – 19 component, not to mention that spray-tanned precedent who has set Amerika back a hundred years or more!!! *WHY WON'T HE JUST SHUT UP?!*

GONE BUT NOT FORGOTTEN

Lyn Lifshin, the self-styled 'Queen of the Small Press' left the planet this year. She was

> *In memory of Maria Fattorini*
> *a beautiful soul*

widely published (LUMMOX Press published a 2 volume set of Little Red Books, The Barbie Poems, back in 1999). I still have copies.

Rudolfo Anaya, A Founding Father Of Chicano Literature.

Michael McClure, one of the last beat poets out of the Bay Area, tapped out earlier this year.

> *In Memory of Ken Greenley*
> *Gone but not Forgotten*

Ken Greenley, committed suicide in Denver, Colorado. I had communicated with him about a week before his departure, but had no idea what was really going on with him.

Steve Dalachinsky died at a NYC poetry reading, I suppose that's a good death for a poet!

L.A. poetry chanteuse, **Yvone de la Vega**, did loopty loops into outer space and was gone! She was a pistol!

> *In Memory of Harry Wilkens*
> *poet and provocateur*

Harry Wilkens passed away this July. Harry and I worked on his book, Piss Talks. His style was raw and visceral.

Milner Place, an English poet & teacher, sailed into the sunset for the last time in late May.

LET US BEGIN...

POETRY I

Austin Alexis

Morning Song

A car horn. Beeping. The emergency alarm, belting out urgency at 7:00 A.M.,
    badgering the winter morning. I sit at my kitchen table, toes cold in my
    slippers. If I will the day to go back to sleep, will it?
A headache begins, above my left eye. In counterpoint to the car honk.
    If the headache were more definite, it would be less trying.
The phone rings. No one ever calls me so early. My cousin's strained voice.
    She tells me that our mutual cousin Jerome passed away last night.
    "Time to mourn," she says, her words riding a sigh.

Matt Amott

Southwest Chief

My car idols
as the crossing gate
comes down for
the oncoming train.

The lights flash
and bells clang along
with Johnny Cash
on the radio and
I think back to
that time he played
on the jukebox,
while we danced
on our first date.

All those promises back then
that neither one of us kept.

I'm brought back
by the rumble of
the train before me.
And when it passes,
the gates lift
and my tires roll over
the rails and on down
the long, empty road
as Johnny's voice
fades from
the radio.

Three by RD Armstrong

In Haiku

It's always
The Moon
In the
Bucket.

Always the
China doll
With porcelain
Skin as pale
And white
As snow.

You never hear
About the tiny
Cracks, or the
Other signs of age.

In Haiku
All is timeless.

It's always
The Moon
In the
Bucket.

Never the
Razor's bite
Or the sting
Of aftershave.

In Haiku

It's always
The Moon
In the
Bucket.

Always the
Ship dissecting
Mt. Fuji's
Calm
Reflection.

Always the
Heron
Taking
Inventory.

Always the
Thoughts of
You turning
In your sleep
Pulling the
Sheets tightly
To your breast.

In Haiku

The kiss lingers
Snow never melts
Rain mists gently
And
The Moon
In the
Bucket
Always holds
Your hopes
And dreams
Waiting for your
Return no
Matter
How long
It takes.

Entropy

Over the past four years
the government clown
has been spinning the plates
like you might see in a circus
one guy running around
6 impossibly slender rods
trying to keep the crockery
up in the air

And the government clown
has been telling us the most
outrageous lies during his tenure
and he's got a lot of people
spellbound watching those plates spin

Meanwhile government goons and
clowns are busy taking everything
that isn't nailed down and stashing
them in huge underground bunkers

And we the spellbound are slowly
catching on we're not that dumb
we hear the scuffling in the background
but the big govt. clown tells us to
watch the plates those goddamned plates
See how they spin, see how the light
bounces off the surface Don't look away
You're helping to keep them spinning
No distractions please Ignore what
you and the pundits think is really
going on just keep watching the plates
Hypnotizing isn't it

Sooner or later the whole distraction
will fail The plates will come crashing
down and chaos will attempt to take over
but chaos may be too sick and tired to
get up and out of the house much less
start anything out on the streets

Even the govt. clown will lose his bluster
and finally become another average Joe
overwhelmed by the realization that even
God cannot keep the plates up and spinning
forever

Menu

Before Covid
Beans and Rice

During Covid
Rice and Beans

After Covid
Beans and Rice

Two by Karen Basiulis

DATELINE MOZAMBIQUE

"Why hasn't anyone come to their
aid?"

Asks the handsome
newscaster

Of no one in
particular.

Floodwaters
rising

Livestock
drowning

People
missing

And women giving birth in
trees.

He does a suave segue into the
local news:

Silicone breast implants
and

The rising cost of
gasoline,

As if he just can't be
bothered

With
people

Who didn't even have the
foresight

To build an
ark.

ASH WEDNESDAY

Remember, if you will, the carnival and the
Man with the sad dirty face
That haunts you still.
You with your mask and feathers
Are strangely attracted to him, like
Dust to a treasured photograph
And you know better than
To blow it away, since you are wearing
the same
Dust that forever seeks out the neglected.
You turn away, but you know you
Will search for him when you
Return, for like the dust,
You will return.

Two by Debbi Brody

Wish Fulfillment

I wished for coyote
And she appeared sauntering down a deer path,

I wished for hawk
And saw osprey, kestrel and red-tail,

I wished for antelope
And saw two small herds,

I wished for Patsy Kline
And the radio played Sweet Dreams of You,

I wished for home
And we arrived before sunset,

I wished for ease and clarity,
Defragmented my mind and found them.

I wished for a map of love
And you lay down beside me.

Empty Nest with Pandemic

The hound howls and our
one outdoor light turns
the orange lid
of the bird feeder neon.

In the backyard, remembering
the times you met me in Bangkok, in
Santiago,
places I never would have gone
had you not been waiting.

We, not confined, not longing
for adventure but keeping
ears wide open for unusual
cries, chirps and singing in
our neighborhood as we review
the adventure of 42 years
with joined hearts,
leaping in and out of fire.

Three by Lynne Bronstein

A Guide to Free Will

Let's not do whatever we want to do.
Not for a while, anyway.
Let us not run through the streets
Or through the grocery aisles.
Let us not fall into temptation.
A hand touched to a hand
Won't make us burn in hell
But it could send us prematurely to heaven.
Let us abide by the sensible rules.
Life is now a comedy of manners
And some things simply are NOT DONE.

But let us do the things we have always dreamed
Of doing
And let us do them in our dreams
Or in that reasonable daytime facsimile of a dream
Called Art.
Let's sing, dance, paint, write, film, video,
And be the best colors and sounds and thoughts
That can fly out of our minds
And be shared without going from hand to hand.
Let us allow our gems to gleam,
To been seen from space
By our not-yet-met friends of the galaxy.
"It's a strange world, this Earth" they will say.
"But it looks like a nice place to visit---
some day."

Desert Thunder (Santa Fe)

Why is the desert thunder so quiet?
Why is the storm so dry?
On one side the sky is blue,
The other, gray,
Pierced with forked lightning.
The storm moves away right before my eyes,
A temporary visitor, as I also am,
Waiting at Santa Fe station.
The storm is a grumbling traveler,
A stranger who can't function
In the thin mountain air.
The storm is
The child in the plaza,
Crying, clenching her fists, lost.
The storm is my
Fatigue, my homesickness,

The conflict of wanting to explore
And wanting to just rest,
The frustration of being hungry
And being unable to chew,
The desire to fulfill desire
While seeking the pleasure of solitude.
All that contradicts
Is embodied in the craziness
Of the blue sky and biting sun on one side,
The dark gray sky and electric glitter on the other.
Seen from a safe distance like a movie screen,
The small, quiet oddball storm
Comes at 4 in the afternoon
And doesn't have the gumption
To stay the night.

Los Angeles On a Day After the Rain

Starbucks eyes
Stare up from the sidewalk.
Wet refuse and leaves
Still scattered.
Don't slip while walking.
The mountains
Can finally be seen
And one can follow
The etchings on their sides,
The fire-trails from the hotter fall.
Be careful to cross
The puddle lake in the parking lot

At its narrowest point.
That puddle called a River
At least looks like a stream today.
The air is full of living aromas,
Grilled tacos on the corner,
A whiff of burning wood.
The city
Has been cleansed.
Now the city
Will turn belly up
To absorb the sun,
To preen itself,

Sexier and more glam,
Until it accumulates
Too much activity,
Stress and stench,
And submits
To dark clouds
That will discharge
Another exemption,
Redemption,
Purgation.
And onward……
For the season.

B.J. Buckley

Eating Seven Pips of a Pomegranate
in Defiance of Winter

The fruits of February
are tight and sweet and small,
the rich dark red of blood
that's settled into the limbs
and begun to cool. Two days ago
all rodent auguries were ambivalent,
contradictory under partly cloudy
heavens soft with thaw – men
in top hats far too squeamish
for consulting entrails, for cutting
anything open. Persephone
was wiser than her years
to take that gut-slashed womb
into her hands, suck the sweet juice
sluicing through her fingers,
tease out pips to feed the wolf
in her belly lest it devour her
will. Seven: snowdrift, sleet-knife,

ice-lock, gale, blizzard, ravens,
burial. Seven pips: and so, I,
against the spell of turncoat
January with its melts and drips.
Last night together cold and darkness
fell and fell and fell, the snow ground glass
against all flesh, and wind a beast
whose claws, like ghosts, could reach
through walls, fierce bird who broke
each branch it rested on. So I,
so nourished, loosed my hair,
went out to marry:
sparrows dropped frozen
from the lilac hedge. Old cottonwoods,
their shattered bones. Blood
where an owl fed.
That flame of ice, my heart.
That flame, the moon.

for Jane Wohl

April Bulmer

Ghost in the Machine

A patient wears a blue mask over her nose and mouth at True North Imaging and
Ultrasound. I watch a flat-screen TV: *The Marilyn Denis Show*. A woman talks
about meditation and mindfulness. A journalist from W5 shares stories from
war-torn Iraq and Mexico. I covet her big black glasses.

A Scottish woman calls my name. I walk the hall behind a man in a short blue gown.
He wears tight black underpants.

The x-ray technician has yellow hair and bad breath. The machine is a god who can
see through my thin skin. It is down; we sit in silence.

Later: Hold your breath, says the woman. The god snaps my photo. He peers like a
child at a window. The technician touches my shoulder. It hurts a little. The god
wants to know if it is broken.

My bones are old now, and there are stories in the marrow. Some of them are sad.

I am a winter tree, my limbs pale. My spirit a kind of sap.

Don Kingfisher Campbell

Dalian Play

A week after lock-down is lifted
People gather in the square
To kick a soccer ball around
Ride bicycles with training wheels
Or just walk together again

This afternoon a blonde doll
In a blue satin dress and
A pink eared white bunny
On all fours sit on a wooden
Park bench ready to eat

The little girl with a pink hat
And blue surgical mask serves
Them slices of plastic pizza
Using a blue plastic shovel
To dish the yellow wedges

The doll falls ill at dinner
The girl places a packet of
Soft cotton cleansing wipes
As a pillow on the red scooter
Rolling as an ambulance

The girl in the pink hat gives
The doll mouth to mouth
While wearing the mask
The bunny at the bench
Doesn't want to eat anymore

Twitches its nose at the small
Boy sporting a black woolen
Ball cap and smaller blue mask
He tries and tries to get bunny
To chew on some faux bread

Meanwhile the doll rests
Eyes closed, her blue shoes
Tethered by a red ribbon
To her wrist dangle under
This nearby hospital bench

The boy comes to visit
Offers dolly a few pine nuts
As medicine for the virus
In what they have named
Wuhan Children's Hospital

Published in The New Verse News

Pris Campbell

Sack Cloth

Hiding my head
under sack cloth,
carving messages of hope
into my bloodied palms,
I cross the seaways you and I
traveled together when we were
still filled with innocence,
before children were slaughtered
at their schools, before young men
strapped on explosives instead of drinking
Kool-Aid for the Rapture,
before an unseen virus entered lungs
and brought life to a standstill.

My knees buckle.
The sky falls, as shrapnel,
around me.

Luis Campos

FOR LEASE

Battered planet -
Still serviceable
but in need of complete overhaul.

-Present occupants' lease
almost up.

-Only children & pets need apply.

Written in 1979

Luis Campos

Two by Alan Catlin

Love Is Colder Than Death

"You have to feel a situation; not hurt someone,
no aggress someone to the point that it's obnoxious,
but accept the fact that you are a voyeur-you're
stealing something from people."
Mary Elen Mark, photographer

They were as amiable as morgue attendants
in the big city on holiday masquerading as humans.
Were as cold shouldered as shark tooth CPA's
who wore their platinum Amex cards in plastic
holders hung on gold chains around their necks
the way hipsters used to wear ARREST ME NOW
razor blades close against overexposed chest hair
with enough residue on thin Wilkinson Sword
edges to generate a warrant to search the house
for more drugs.
Were prey to every hustler that ever ran a fleet
of underage orphans working off debts on
their backs, learning a trade they'd be too old
for by the time they could legally buy a drink.
Would have souvenirs of their raise hell week,
on the loose, clinicians would shake their heads
over saying, "Haven't seen strains of VD like
that since the Black Plague, R&R boys used to
bring back from the Nam."
Had children who wouldn't look out of place
among the cast of *Freaks* or who spent their
brief lives in Homes for Demented Children.
Might live well into their 40's before an untimely
death. They are rarely mourned.

Escape from New York

Down and out in some east village
other pad, when it was hip.
Ignoring the loose stairs, the gang
symbols, morgue shift graffiti,
tapped-a-vein blood splash walls.
Whole neighborhoods gone, like
wasted, man, crazy with hop heads,
white powder dippers, lsd banditos,
day tripping well beyond strawberry
fields forever. Avoiding the Benzedrine
cowboys with guitars, all the manic
rockers: unwashed, unhinged, unfocused.....
All the Sunday bloody Sunday psalms,
the Solomon solution songs, the near-death
babies in woven straw baskets left
in derelict doorways. All the 'no one
knows what trouble I've seen' lyrics;
six months old and already past his prime.
Mail bombs and anthrax love potions,
the poisoned powdered stabbed through
the heart valentine, with a cryptic, apocalypse
now, inscription "Thinking of you"
and signed by Charlie M and the Family.
Blood brother handprints on every apartment
wall: Death to Pigs, final notices on
kicked in, no lock doors. Post haste,
no return address left, leaving town exit.
No looking back. What would be the point?

Grace Cavalieri

View

My sacred space, a bird flying to the feeder
the shade of a tree, berries in the forest
heat from the sun on the pane
flames of experience
lashing on glass
the clear path of vision
the straight edge of sky
a parting of water
picking us up placing us exactly there
history has been shattered into pieces that will not fit together
how large is loss
how much does it take to fill
how do we gather it in our arms
when the city was destroyed with illness there was a place I could not reach
right now a small animal is breaking free in the woods
the milk of the moon is shining on these words that come from me
and do not return empty.

Jonathon Church

Kin, Blues, and Laughs

An old graybeard poet
wrinkled to the bone
by years of grit, smoke, and drink –
kin, blues, and laughs –
hobbles over to his "thinking chair"
by the window.

He lights a match,
then a candle.
He feels a breeze slip
under the crack
of a windowsill
and get lost
in the dark room.

The candle's flame
shivers,
but endures.
Candle shrinking,
wax melting away
imperceptibly.

Shadows leap onto the wall
like voices from the oblivion
of the poet's scarred reminiscence.
They are dragged
back to the floor
by the solemn gaze
of the steady flame…

sinking

sinking

sinking

like a boat with a small leak
before it capsizes,
Ahab on the deck
staring at the stars,
sea breezes
grazing his neck
like the tap
of a grim reaper
rising from the ocean,
black maw ready
to feast on shipwrecks
and the last gasps
of desperate lungs
and failing hearts,
all out of kin,
all out of blues,
all out of laughs,
dreading the abyss,
before drowning
in the music of Sirens
calling them home
for the last time.

Ed Coletti

Refugees

Someone else's little boy
walking immediately behind

I arrive at the final check point
am insistently waved through

I want nothing more in the world
only to simply cross over

Certainly not change to salt
looking back at the child

All I have left to me is
my ability to rationalize

At best for me on the other side
stretch twenty declining years

seventy or eighty for him
But I am not this child's keeper am I

He has my sympathy: From him I have
the burn of his eyes on my reddening neck

all the more so as I admit to myself
I am not helpless before this determined little kid

Here in the presence of real human suffering
All I have left: clear choice and ability to justify

Sharyl Collin

Reluctant Savior

There is a tickle on my cheek
just below the rim of my mask.
I try to ignore it as I walk
the deserted street. Clouds clear
as the sun dries rain
from the blacktop,

his business uninterrupted
by the virus that has set humans
on edge. Cast in the crosshairs
of a fickle assassin, we're given
too much information
that is still not enough.

They tell us when to a wear
a mask, how to disinfect
the groceries and give us links
to apply for unemployment,

while our president mocks
the counsel of his advisors
and recommends a cocktail
of bleach. And no one
can agree on how or when
we can move on.

I'm afraid it's a journey like that
of an Alzheimer's patient,
with each day taking more
while I lose my will
and embrace the forgetful haze.

I process the image of an earthworm
writhing on the sidewalk
after I've passed it. I declare
to myself that I won't go back.
'This is the new me," I insist,
while my conscience churns
to life. 'You have always

saved the worms. If not you,
then who?" I resent her intrusion
into my forgetful haze.
'I don't care,' I insist, but she
just smiles as I pivot

and retrace my steps. I hope
that no one is watching
as I lift the worm
from the sidewalk.
I set it in the dirt,
praying that it
can return to a normal life.

Two by Pat Connors

Becoming

it is always becoming a poem
this furnace, this fire
in a corner of the body's dark

this is the place that burns
whatever has been broken

"Heart", by Mick Burrs

The world says
we are the result
of the residue
it leaves upon us.

Don't let this be.
Burn this dross from me!
No matter the pain it brings
I will not be like everyone else.

Mold me in your image
form me in the refiner's crucible
that my thoughts, my work
and my poetry may bring you glory.

Let all the indescribable pain
endured while becoming understandable
bring clarity to my vision
and integrity to my life.

Then my words would blaze
a trail across the midnight sky
and be a likeness of the light
which will forever shut out darkness.

Pantoum

The smouldering fire of his heart
stoked by hope borne of a long wait
was yet truly the very start
of uncovering such a trait.

Stoked by hope borne of a long wait
he learns the truth within the dream
of uncovering such a trait
beauty greater than what may seem.

He learns the truth within the dream
the radiant light in his eyes
beauty greater than what may seem
coaxing his desire to arise.

The radiant light in his eyes
was yet truly the very start
coaxing his desire to arise
the smouldering fire of his heart.

Chris Cressey

The Long Goodbye

each day I awake and ask myself
will it be today?
will this be the day I realize there can be no more putting off the inevitable
as a lifelong steward of animal care I pride myself on the years of excellent
beast parenting I have provided

G. Murray Thomas

yet as signs become more apparent I have trouble
drawing a line between when this current dog
has suffered more than enjoyed
I ask myself how much procrastination is for me
she has been deaf and blind the better part of
the past five years adapted to three substantial
moves in four years in spite of her disabilities
endured the loss of her familiar habitat and
constant companion from childhood
how will I know when she has endured enough
how will I be able to choose the day to end it
how will I survive without her

xj Dailey

GET SMARTER IN 5 MINUTES

for Scooter

It's reversal of fortune cookie, a failure to inundate, it's emotional bandwidth cowering
under the bandstand, it's 106 degrees, it's palm trees swaying, it's mud flap pop tart just
off the pathological (follicles @ dawn), it's gingerly sidestepping the downpour, the uproar,
the upshot, the shot put, it's beer-battered duck leg, infallible fluctuation sustained (so
far) by bluff, it's the it's the endorphins accompanied by smiling dolphins, it's this short-
lived longevity, Jasper, it's thoughtlessness or mindfulness, it's EVERY SINGLE LEAF
ATTACHED TO EACH INEFFABLE LIMB airing right before MAKE ROOM FOR
CORRUPTION OF THE TEXT, it's chopper down, heliport with excuses overgrown,
it's kitchen utensils in revolt, subdivisions by long division, it's pet skeptical, 'tis a
consummation devoutly to be torpedoed by lint, release this into the Wild as soon as

Two by Micheal Estabrook

It's nice that's all

So you sent your first
real book of poems
to half a dozen respected
well-known poets and one of them –
Ron P. still active
dozens of books under his belt –
sent a return email to you:
"Thank you very much for sending me your book
which I enjoyed, and for your poem about Larry
which I also enjoyed.
What a wonderful grump he was!"

So now you're on "cloud nine"
a real poet knows who you are.
So? So what!
You can't expect anything substantial
to result from one
measly 28 word email
from one "famous" poet can you?
Are you delusional? And
if something were to result, what might that be?

So don't start thinking you're a big shot
because really you're not
the Devil assures me
wagging a gnarled, bony, cautionary finger.

The Great Depression

Yes, you lose sleep
worrying where the money
will come from
for the new septic system
and to pay the credit card debts
and to fly to Florida to visit your mother.

I know you worry. I'm sorry about that.
But you have come
from so much more dire circumstances
from so much worse –
the Grandfather who in the Great Depression
slept in his car with his three daughters
ate spaghetti and stale bread
who dug ditches and graves
and drove a laundry truck
to keep his family together
after their mother
left her life on the kitchen floor
in desperation and despair.

So you see I cannot feel sorry for you
you have a 60 inch TV
iPhones iPads computers and the Internet
music and a subscription to the Boston Lyric Opera
a medical plan and a house cleaner
you have been to Hawaii, London and Paris
you eat fresh fruits and vegetables
and steak
and sleep in a bed.

Mark Evans

Poetisa

The poet, the *cigana*
on her return from the beach
unpretentiously approaches.
Underneath a *lua* and *Vênus*,
she is in full bloom
wet jeans holding souvenirs of sand
she saunters side to side, up curb
and down - slinky and playful
on this poorly lit street
like something untethered
too much wine
boots and journal in hand.

With not quite a stumble,
she smiles with portentous Portuguese lips,
her eyes and gaze the depth of some acute ancient wisdom.
She murmurs to herself, and then tightly grabs my shirt.
Pulling me close as she passes by
she whispers—with a gritty, de minimis softness:

"There is nowhere to go but forward,
maybe you don't ask the questions,
simply because you don't want to know the answers,
but they do not care how many suffer
as long as their agenda is fulfilled."

Hand to her mouth, giggling, she muffles a slightly enticing,
seemingly omniscient—if not somewhat malevolent—laugh,
and disappears into the mist of an adjacent alley.
We are now, somehow, connected strangers,
somewhere between the tick and the tock of some synchronous clock.

After the breakup, I retreat into Sappho at my usual diner

Beneath crusty topping, the cheddar and noodles—a long blonde hair. This is no accident. It's a call for help, and me, too morose to hear. The long, blonde waitress reads over my shoulder, waits for my credit card, plays with her split ends. She points at my book, asks, *Who's Sappho?* When I tell her 'a poet from ancient Greece', she rolls her eyes. *Me? I like noir. Ever read any Elmore Leonard? Jim Thompson?* she asks. *The Killer Inside Me?* She attacks the crumbs on my table. I'm not sure what she wants. *Is that what you've got?* I ask her. *A killer inside you?* The waitress shrugs. *Don't we all?* She strikes too close to home. When I don't answer, she tries again. *Maybe you should be reading something relevant, writing about, fuck, I dunno, slow death at a greasy spoon?* When I look surprised, she gets in my face. *I see you here, every day, same table, writing in that notebook, always alone. What? Real life's too real for ya? Gotta retreat to ancient history?* She's got my number. The waitress picks up my plate. *Jim Thompson'd tell you, women are like crockery. Chipped*, she says. *Disposable. Even your precious Sappho.* She points at the glistening fat beading off my abandoned mac and cheese. *Greece? I'll show you ancient grease.* She palms my credit card, brings it to the cashier. *Who broke you?* I ask, when she returns with my receipt. Incredulous, the waitress looks to see who's listening, then leans in. *The same losers who broke you.*

First published in Petrichor, 2019

Domestic Violence

Knives cut both bread and throats, he warns, the stiletto's steel tip teasing my trachea. A love tap. I'm used to it. I don't react anymore; I bake. I knead, pound the dough instead of him. Each day when he leaves for court, those $2,000 suits camouflaging his viciousness, a brief reprieve. I envision his face in the smacked-down dough, push out the air pockets, dream of suffocation. I slap him, punch him, only to watch him rise. While he proofs, I look for loopholes, binge-watch *Forensic Files*, its endless stories of stymied desire, hour after hour of scheme and kill, each murder more gruesome, honed. I take notes, stick in a shiv to see if he's done, plot that he comes to a similar bad end. I shape loaves like alibis, knife-notched before they go into the oven, frenzied jabs and slices. I sharpen the blade, ready for his return. Like him, I'll never speak without a lawyer present.

First Published in UNSHEATHED Anthology, 2019

Joseph Farley

Stalagtus

My loneliness is not
your loneliness.
We stare at each other
across a precipice.

What we see
and what we feel
may seem the same,
but it is not.

Even the vultures circling
can tell the difference
although they can't put it
in words.

Stay to your pile of rock.
I'll stay on mine.
We'll both dream
of other, better things.

But I will not dream
of you,
and you will not dream
of me,

and the sun will not forget
to rise each day
to bleach our bones white
for our reluctance.

Raindog

Two by Sarah Ferris

A Mare's Swagger

I like a mare's swagger,
up and down of head
as feet move in tandem,
ripple of muscles, flick of tail.
Mares gleam in the sun,

doin' their thing, moving
through their day
the way I own the sidewalk,
poised and self-possessed—
until I register

the third time a man's look
follows me. Then I wonder
whether there's spinach
between my teeth or
my makeup smeared and I

stumble, inside, for just a minute.
But on sunny days,
I walk my mare-swagger,
on sunny days, I walk heart-first,
and sparkling palm fronds wave

as though to catch my attention
with their double time glee.
on sunny days, I notice
sunbeams on water, a dog's
wagging tail. That's the great thing

about being on the sidewalk
in sunlight, the windows
don't reflect, whereas
on cloudy days, I see my
reflection and all that I judge.

My Lover

When he passes me I don't see grey hair—
I feel his arms around me and hear whispered words.
His hand trails across my back,
down around my curves—
making promises to my senses.

When he lectures our daughter
on the importance of doing the work first,
she leans forward on her elbows
eyes follow him
from the fridge to the cutting board to the stove,

attention fixed on him like a perfectly tuned string
which his words run up and down
like an Eric Clapton rift.
I walk quietly then, listening
to the melody between them.

When he passes by
I do not see a round, softened belly.
I remember the day before,
the throw from third base to first, that broke
the laces of the first baseman's glove.

My lover passes by,
the back of his hand caresses my cheek,
slides down around and opens behind my neck.
Cradling my head with his irresistible touch
he reminds me that I am his and he is mine.

Gwendolyn Fleischer

OASIS OF SENSATION

Souls merge and crash
   in darkest night
Ocean waves
Fierce flashes of light
I am born anew
   in midnight moonlight
Tested to the edge

Beyond the brink
Explosions so deep
   I cannot think
Nothing I see for I have become
Sensations and sound
Eyes with heavy lids
Nothing else is around
Totally absorbed
   in the ebb and flow
Into this brand new world I soar

I am struck to my very core
Eagerly awaiting
   what else is in store
Fall into arms warms with desire

Falling into stars
Crashing into meteors
Tasting succulent
   sweet strawberry kisses
Shivering touches
Floating to the ends of the universe
Ice cold on the tongue
Hot moist breath dissolves
Electric surges
Fingers' light touches
Every fiber vibrating with life
And disappear weak kneed
Into the cosmic intertwining

Dennis Formento

Only love can bring back courage or else despair

"... live as 'beatific
Spirits welded
together'"
-- Ed Sanders

"Only love can bring back courage or else despair"
and create something mystical out of mud
Dude says, "somebody just shot me in the head!
I can't pay attention to that! YOU pay attention to that!"
So I crawl 150 feet to the next gas station
the air is thick with smoke
acrid with bad science
but what took us into this must walk us back out again
there is no receding into tomorrow. Brother says
"Cop just shot me in the back of the head!
Won't somebody PLEASE help me get onto my feet
and into the emergency room … that ain't there no more?"
If we had no future tense, would we
have come this far, would we
live longer without that?
Brother says,
"You all got us into this mess, now you got
to get us all out of it. Do I look like I started this?"
I'm shifting weight from foot to foot, like

I got to find a place to pee
He's got a point there, but
how many people in my vicinity
actually profit from all of this cancer?
rising water crowds
the feet of plants and they drown, roots
salty with the intruding Gulf.
Oh, but summer's just dawning
and its teeth are grinding, glaring
down upon the fleet
of taxicabs stuck in traffic
on the rooftop bridge.
I'm going upstairs among the clouds
to bed
Summer's coming & the whole damn mess
is crawling over Elevator Hill.

And it's taking with it
all the people who can afford not to think
about it

Previously published by Unlikely Stories (online) Nov. 2018

Bill Gainer

The Purpose of the Little Garage

Been building a
little garage
in the back.

Actually
it's a little room
with a big door
a window
and a little
door
that open
to the world.

I wish to sit there
someday
sip my bourbon
enjoy the rocks
out front
the movement of time
and the quiet.

Not silence.
Silence is scary
but the quiet –

The quiet
is when time
holds you
peacefully
in its hand
extends its thumb
to set your glass on.

The birds, bugs
and other things
sometimes
nothing
stop by
in a whisper
wish you well
and leave.

Raindog

Two by William Scott Galasso

Rise Up

Rise up young people! Rise with loud voice, fresh spirit,
stout hearts, carry your signs, flags, banners, waving
in crowded streets, march out of step with elder
complacency, strike with righteous indignation before
you're left scorched earth, drowned cities, barren
hills, poisoned air, water suffused with lead.

Rise up, contest the lies of iniquitous politicians
who barter your future for Big Business bucks
or abase themselves to NRA patrons putting
bulls-eyes on your backs. Rise up, open deaf
ears give sight to those refuse to see. Create
the world you hunger for, this is your job, our
hope, your time.

Rise up with Greta Thunberg*, David Hogg,
Jacklyn Corin! Rise up with Emma Gonzalez
and Alex Wind, to whom silence holds no virtue
just betrayal of their dead.

And remind those in whose footsteps you follow
that once they marched for peace, for justice
for the right to stand equal before God despite
gender, color or whomever they chose to love.
Rise up young people tweak the conscience
of those who sleep. Rise up, Rise up!

**Greta Thunberg, teenage climate activist
who spoke at the UN. David, Jackyn, Emma
and Alex are Parkland students and gun control
advocates.*

Four On Cityscape

*(Edward Hopper,
American Painter 1882-1967)*

Hopper's Nighthawks
who has not been, one alone
half in shadow
coffee cup cradled in hand
in a city full of strangers

a man and woman
sit at opposite tables
they don't engage
Sunlight in a Cafeteria
silence fills the room

Automat in oil
nineteen twenty-seven
a woman, not old
fixates on her cup 'a joe
if her eyes met yours, what then?

a *Room in Brooklyn*
windows filter morning light
a woman in blue
sits in a wooden rocker
miles of roof tops before her

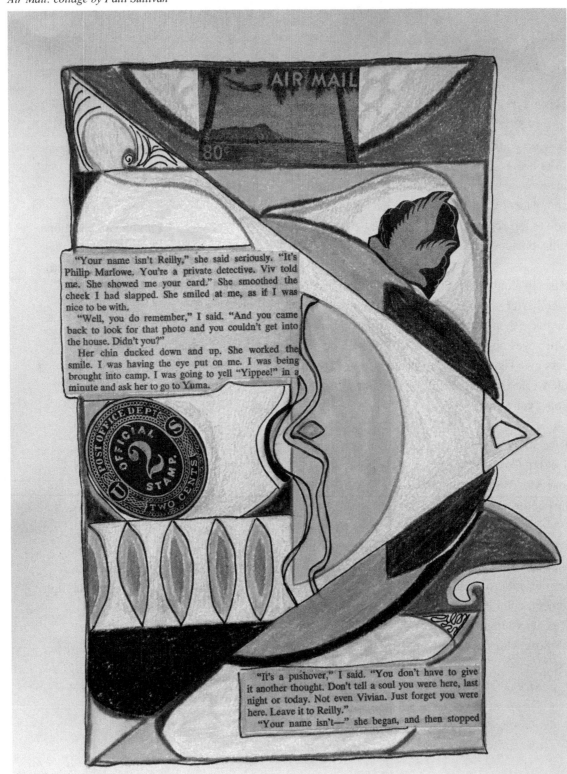

"Your name isn't Reilly," she said seriously. "It's Philip Marlowe. You're a private detective. Viv told me. She showed me your card." She smoothed the cheek I had slapped. She smiled at me, as if I was nice to be with.

"Well, you do remember," I said. "And you came back to look for that photo and you couldn't get into the house. Didn't you?"

Her chin ducked down and up. She worked the smile. I was having the eye put on me. I was being brought into camp. I was going to yell "Yippee!" in a minute and ask her to go to Yuma.

"It's a pushover," I said. "You don't have to give it another thought. Don't tell a soul you were here, last night or today. Not even Vivian. Just forget you were here. Leave it to Reilly."

"Your name isn't—" she began, and then stopped

Martina Robles Gallegos

Enough Already!

When it pours, it rains. No kidding! It's the flood of the century!
I'd like to see the floods cease before I dig my own grave.
No. I ain't digging. I'll be cremated and floods sent to Mercury.
I feel like a coward though others call me brave.

I thought I'd sown gentle, loving, caring seeds
just like my humble mother did,
so why am I harvesting awful, hating weeds?
I'd like to know where my efforts hid.

Why do I cry when I'm supposed to laugh
and laugh when I'm supposed to cry?
Wasn't almost dying enough?
Doesn't anybody see me try?

Every day my thoughts are foggier than a summer
morning in my native town.
Every bright day makes me wonder:
will I stand next day, or will I die sitting down?

Whether I die or whether I live,
I know I did the best I could
and gave all I could give.
My heart's made of muscle and not wood.

All those sad thoughts screaming in my head
want to fly free before they cause any harm.
'Cause sometimes sad thoughts can make you dead,
or they may cause a broken arm.

I was one to grab the bull by the horn,
but now I'm tired of the bullshit!
Everything in me is now torn.
There's not a damn thing that can fix it!

So, enough already, I said!
Stop all the madness now before it's late!
I refuse to end up dead
before I give this fragile world a second take.

Two by J. W. Gardner

CRACKER BOX

Small town memories of
Small town mentalities of
The Dirty Oakie White Trash
Way of life
  In The Cracker Box
  We got
Kool-Aid in the milk jug
Spam in the frying pan
And everyone sporting
That mid-summer
Overalls farmer's tan
  In The Cracker Box
  We got
Yards full of tow headed babies
In nothing but diapers
Old folks sipping beer and whisky
On couches on front porches
Telling the children that will still listen
About the harrowing trip escaping
The Oklahoma Dust Bowl nightmare in '34
  In the Cracker Box
  We got
A broke down Chevy Nova
And a Ford Maverick with no wheels
Lined up on the dead lawn
Ready for the kids
To race imaginary NASCAR
And there's about a dozen dogs
Laying under the willow tree shade
Lying next to my drunk uncle
With a broken wrench and an empty bottle
Singing he's damn sure got it made

  In The Cracker Box
  We got
Chickens and pigs
And rabbits in hutches
Even a goat out back
Next to the hand me down clothes
Drying on the clothes line
Fenced away from the vegetable garden
Hiding the marijuana plants
Hung up and drying in the old wooden shack
  In The Cracker Box
  We got
The church people coming through
Bringing bags of food
And winter clothes
Even a couple pair of shoes
  In the Cracker Box
  We got
Chops cooking on the homemade grill
Corn and potatoes wrapped in foil
Buried in the coals like the three cases of PBR
Buried in a trash can full of ice
With Lynard Skynard and Merle Haggard
Even old George Jones and David Alan Coe
Blasting from speakers hard wired into
The old Pioneer SX-1980 radio

IDIOT WISDOM

        In The Cracker Box
        We got
Shirtless teenage boys
Sporting homemade tattoos
Trying to impress the teenage girls
In cut off jean shorts and halter tops
By shooting beer cans with .22s
Smoking hand rolled Bugler tobacco
While talking about
The big things they're gonna do
When they figure out
How to break out
Never understanding
That this is how
The end always begins
        In The Cracker Box
        You got
Your baby on her hip and another on the way
Life time of day labor
And thank God for the food stamps
Double wide living
        In The Cracker Box

P.O.S. Maverick
Painted with brushes
Suitcase latches
Holding the roof in place
Three on the tree
1st gear don't engage
Four bald tires and no spare
No jack no star
Just a bent rusty screwdriver
Stuck in the ignition
Rolling down the country road
Going to the country store
Going to use the telephone
Going to get some change
On the food stamps
Cash in the cans in the trunk of the Maverick
To get some sodas and beer
Maybe a pack of Kool King Cigarettes
Heading back to cinder block cube called home
Nestled between a cow pasture and rice paddy
Crossed by giant endless horizon to horizon
Corn fields filled
With wise and cruel magical scarecrows
Holding court
Endlessly laughing mocking
Taking
Such glee
In our misery
Always there whispering in the wind
There is no escape
No escape
Like the rabbit in the jaws of the wolf
Field mouse in the curved raptor's talon
The secrets of idiot wisdom

Tony Gloeggler

DETROIT

When you step up to the ticket window,
the sweet smiling sexy twenty year old
hands you your ticket and change, says
she likes your shirt, a deep purple tee
with a print of an Indian chief on horseback,
his war-bonneted head raised high, leaning
back triumphantly, arms spread wide
taking the whole world in and celebrating
the Beach Boys, fifty years of harmony.
You stand there, wonder how weird
it would be to dub her a mixed CD
of Brian's little known gems. You'd joke,
explain that you are part of an official
musical mission and all women as beautiful
as she should have a little holiness sprinkled
in with her *fun fun fun*. As you walk in,
she tells you their songs never grow old,
unlike you, who is trying not to imagine
her undressing, your hands lightly cupping
the curve of her ass. It's a mid week matinee
and the theater is nearly empty. You could sit
in the back row, jerk off if you wanted to,
but the movie is *Detroit* and the smooth,
shiny Motown grooves of the Temptations,
Martha and her Vandellas, Marvin, Tammi,
fill in every background lull and build up
tension when *A Little Bit Of Soul* slips in,

brings you back to Queens, stickball in the street,
throw it up and hit a Spaldeen two sewers long
while Eddie Berne's band rehearsed, singing
You gotta make like you wanna kneel and pray
And then a little bit of soul will come your way
over and over in his garage for Friday night's
St Ann's dance. Jackie, the third best player
in the neighborhood is starting to sprout tits.
She'd probably laugh, make a face or punch
you in the shoulder if you asked her to dance
or mentioned anything about her sister sitting
on her porch, strapped to a wheelchair,
spastically waving her arms and moaning
the day away. At thirteen, you didn't know
anyone black. Everyone was Irish or Italian
or Jewish. A Chinese guy owned the laundry.
Sometimes you'd stand in the doorway,
make deep loud guttural sounds until
he came out shaking his fists and yelling
gibberish as you ran down the block, out
of breath, and laughing. Back on the screen,
Detroit is burning. The cops closed down
an all black after hours spot, piled everyone
into vans as a simmering crowd gathered.
The colored folks went crazy and the police
went crazier and everyone knows the cops
will get away with everything in the end.

First Published in Pittsburgh Poetry Review

Drought

I have brought my iced tea upstairs where I sit on the wood chair at
the bedroom window, so I can get a good view of the neighbor's yard.

On that side of the fence are flowers grown fat with
love and water these many months, while in my yard
sunflowers droop and even the dandelions wither.

I sigh.

My neighbors and their ignorant flowers use too much.
This flagrant waste will bring the end to daisies and petunias,
to pansies and dahlias, to fruit trees and rose bushes.

As the ice in my mint tea melts, the
clammy glass slips from my grasp. I peel
my sweaty thighs from the seat of the chair,
and let them fall back onto a drier spot.
I ignore the spilled tea. I stare out the window.

Virtuous and certain in my self-denial,
I drink in the beauty next door.

In the Broken Light, In Owl Weather

from Colloquy, Weldon Kees

Branches turn the
moon off turn the
moon on. Windows
rattle.

The barn owl leaves her nestlings. No
sound, no sound, no sound, no sound
from her wings spread wide.

The field mouse doesn't stand a chance,
its little panic drowned out by the shush
shush of branches.

She comes back with her prize.
The young are fed, and oh how
hungry they are. She turns away
again, silent, graceful her swoop,
her hunt, her work, her hunger.

Art Goodtimes

Cancer Novena

I remember the rituals of St. Joe's
as sensory overloads

God bread wafers melting on the tongue
The scents of frankincense & burning beeswax
Widor's 5th Symphony organ crescendos

Choristers
like cloud yachts
cup-racing in a storm

Though 'tis true some of
seminary's memory icons
photograph paint-pealed & shabby

Ordeals
Like having to endure the obligatory
kneeler shin bruise from that other Alioto
at the end of our class's long six-latiner pew

Getting dunked in the jakes
Head stuffed down a urinal for a scary
minute or more -- or less, to the hazer's mood

Or fighting to keep awake & not yawn
through interminable medieval ballets of
gold embroidered chasubles & *kyrie eleisons*
in languages on resuscitation from another age

Funeral rosaries led by the clergy
And those passion play Stations of the Cross
devotionals
The altar boys swinging smoking censers

Except in the Grotto
where doing ritual in nature
felt right. Deliciously distracting

Given this medical cancer odyssey
adventure, ordeal
I now find myself on
In

Which I know others of you
have done & are doing
I'm surprised to discover
the gifts this dis-ease brings

My daughters & sons rally around me

A poet offers me a room where
the ceiling glows with stars when the lights go out
in the city of my six-weeks treatments

Everyone agreeing to let me shirk obligations
& responsibilities & sometimes even basic chores
as though I had done them a favor

Getting a fairy godmother treasure chest of salves
& nitrile gloves. Fleece-lined wool socks.
Goodies & glitter

Others gifting me painted
rocks. Icons. Old photos. Invoking litanies
of books. Cannabis oil. Thousands of cards and texts
Tapes, memes, prayers and mailings

The cyber grace of 900+ friends
from around the world
sending their support

And, McRedeye sez
he ain't even dead yet

ART GOODTIMES

Lone Cone Broadside   *Union of Mountain Poets*
Vincent St. John Local / Headwaters of Maverick Draw / Aztlán
Jack Mueller Brigade / Western Slope / 4 Corners
Kuksu Brigade (Ret.) / San Francisco
13020

Two by Tony Gruenewald

The Later Middle Ages

This is the Age of Knowing...
–Tagline from a pharmaceutical ad

This is the age of knowing
That when I walk
Through the waiting room
The cable news channel
Will be airing
A commercial
From some law firm
Fishing for clients
That claim harm
From the med that's
Meant to ensure me
Against an eternity of
Waltzing down hospital halls
In a backless gown, with
An IV pole partner.

This is the age of knowing
That despite its litany
Of risks
When the concerned
Pharmacist asks,
"You know this prescription costs..."
An amount that could induce
A medical emergency in itself
I have no option
But to shrug and say,
"It beats the alternative."

This is the age of knowing
The music I grew up with
Has grown too old
For even the oldies station
Programmed to numb
The medically-induced anxiety
Of the pharmacy's
Targeted demographic.

This is the age of knowing
The pretty faces on
The cover of the gossip rag
At the checkout
Declared to be
The sexiest people alive are
Not only totally
Foreign to me
But appear to be
Younger than my children.

And *this is the age of knowing*
That the next time
anyone will market to me again
Is when it
Finally has
My Medicare dollars
To squander.

The Substitute

The son of my father
Is the Son of God
Again

And he's about to be
Crucified
For the second time
This Palm Sunday

As I act as
My congregation's
Stand-in Paschal Lamb,

Sacrificed to save
This fallen humanity
Of which I'm
A most sinful
Member-in-full.

While we re-
Enact The Passion
I hear

The stand-in Judas,
Peter, Pilate, and
Once-hosanna-hing mob

Betray, deny, and
Condemn me,

Like the Nazis
And a complicit
Christian Europe

Betrayed, denied
And condemned
My father's family.

And though
This not-quite-Semite
Is just a substitute

King of the Jews,
I feel I've failed
My flock;

As I'm struck again
They scatter,
Millennia after millennia,
Fallen over and over
Over and over…

Tom Gannon Hamilton

Gateway

Portal or barrier, depending
on whether the visitor is invited or not;
a decade went by without a break;
enough grease to quell any complaint,
I made nary a squeak, then
violent winds bent my hasp and hinges.

At length and every angle,
with fingers, hands, arms, in torsion,
torque was applied by the proprietor
to fix the flaws,
reverse the ridges, ripples, wrinkles,
undo the furrows, alas, to no avail;
brute sinew couldn't bend them back.

Only when clamped in that rude
steel vice: your unsmiling linear mouth,
would those plates flatten,
did my metal straighten out again;
mine is not a nice, genteel gratitude;
but it's as real as my welcome.

Two by Vijali Hamilton

Boeing 777

Here we are in the air
like a bird of freedom,
man's longed for dream.
Yet are we thrilled—no.

As the plane takes flight
we ask for newspaper,
eat pretzels, drink wine,
then snore away time

as if it wasn't a miracle
that we have wings
and are finally air born--
our dream come true.

Oh soul, you forget
as our fingers press the button
and the movies start, setting
other desires into motion.

And we drift into death
snoring into infinity
with our dream of wings
our dream of freedom

forgotten.

On flight to India, 2020

LYON WOMAN

In the fields of life
I have made myself strong
as a lion, beautiful of face.
Sun giver of life, flame of fire,
come forward in my body,
my own divine house. You are
more than the light in temples,

You are my strength inside.

I have made transformations
all at the dictates of my heart.
With my name upon water
may I join Thee who made
me come into being.

I wait for the season of ripening.

With gifts I come before you
to walk among the living.
Come to the fields of life,
lay your grief upon my body.
Come, let us make for ourselves
an hour lying down among trees
and stones and a running brook--
our mouths to the earth rejoicing.

Let us live in the company of flames.
2020

*Inspired by the Egyptian Book of the Dead and
my time in Egypt, 1989. Egypt was a difficult
country for me. Traveling alone as a single
woman I was attacked twice. A divine force
rose out of myself to protect my life. From the
strength I felt, this song rose to my lips.*

Brian D'Amage

Michael Hathaway

How It Happens

The State declared him "disabled,"
but he is super smart and loves books and history.
He is dysfunctional in life and sorely awkward in social situations.
He doesn't fit anywhere
except somewhere on the Autism Spectrum.
In the harsh real world,
he isn't welcome too many places, not even family reunions –
but in the museum research library that I manage,
anyone who loves books is royalty.
He never approaches me, just goes straight to the books.
He's so near-sighted he holds the books
right up to his round granny specs to read.
His long hair is turning white.
He's big and round like Santa Claus.
He even dresses as Santa might dress at home
on the other 364 days –
perennial plaid, bright primary colors,
and the ever-present red suspenders.
He is eccentric, but so Victorian polite.
He seldom speaks, but when he does
it's with such earnestness,
such over-succinct enunciation.
His sentences are punctuated with pauses,
he pronounces each syllable
as if he invents the words as he speaks –
as if all creation hangs on a Word.
One
Morning
I was so much busier than usual in the library,
with researchers from other states,
and local folks researching genealogy.
Many scholars demanded assistance
as I rushed about in all the four directions.

He appeared in the midst of all this chaos,
and for the first time ever,
marched with purpose right up to my counter,
wearing an enigmatic, self-satisfied grin,
an omnipotent gleam in his eye.
With grand pomp and ceremony,
he held out an upturned fist,
and unfurled his fingers to reveal a perfect robin's egg.
"For you," he said.
I thought, So this is how it happens.
Everyday-Santa just appears in the primordial void,
sporting John Lennon's specs and Mona Lisa's smile,
holds Brahmanda in the palm of his Orphic hand,
Pangu pops out
before you can even say big bang.

(Published in Chiron Review #109, fall, 2017, and two 2019 Spartan Press books by the author: Talking to Squirrels and Postmarked Home: New and Selected Poems 1979-2019.)

George Held

The Distance

"Begin"—not the most promising
    verb

for the new sexagenarian,
who's happy just to wake up
and begin another day,
to learn the day's news,

to marvel at the president's
new tweets,
to check the new emails
and to measure the distance
between here and then.

Debbie Okun Hill

Vapor Lock on the Corner of 7th and B

On this hot day, I've only stopped for a minute
but now the old Ford won't start. Vapor lock.
I crank the windows down and wait for the engine to cool.

Across the street is a house I wish my grandmother lived in,
gray clapboard, big front veranda framed by white pillars.

There's a porch swing for talk or lovers after dark.
A dappled cat to patrol the rose garden.

Next to the hitching post stand two ancient elms.
I gaze into their topmost branches where the sun
patterns the leaves, like looking up through water.

My body relaxed,
my limbs become weightless,
I float in cool green,

My breath forms
bubbles that rise

one
at a time
and bloom . . . .

Lori Wall-Holloway

Win for the Day

It is the popular game show
in the 1960's - *Let's Make a Deal*
Crazily dressed hopefuls are in line
waiting to be chosen to be on TV
shouting to the staff, "Pick me! Pick me!"
A mother of five with long dark hair
dressed in a jumpsuit covered
with eye catching yellow
and orange flowers, says, "Oh forget
it. You're not going to pick me."
Immediately, the man turns
to her and says, "You!"

Carrying a large purse full
of stuff the host might ask
for, a crew member seats
the woman in one of two
front rows in the audience
behind the floor where contestants
play for various prizes until
the end when the big deal is made

She observes the filming of the action
below her until the credits start to roll
That is when Monte Hall quickly begins
to move amongst the spectators and offers
money for specific belongings that may
be in a person's possession

He approaches her with a smile and says
"I'll give you $100 for a stamped envelope!"
Rummaging in her bag, she immediately
pulls out an envelope with a colorful airmail stamp
yelling, "Here!"

 "You've got a deal!" he responds

Overwhelmed, my mom gratefully
took the $100 she just won

Rehanul Hoque

Beauty

Beauty is a word found from the pink
Of a Flamingo
Everyone loves pink
There is no color of the graves
Of brine shrimp!

Two by Ilhem Issaoui

Sadness has laughter

Loud
Louder than that of mirth
Haaa-pahhhh
Voices unheard, you see?
Aren't we all
But fetuses awaiting death
Waiting for life to abort us
We feel the abortion when we stop and think

And hence ignoring it
Being silly and nonchalant
Is but a fleeting entertainment
To divert us for a moment
From the thought that
We are on our way
We are on our way
Live! Live! We say
With two sticks resembling fingers
We draw a silly smile
And they believe
That we are brimming with mirth
Swimming and snuffling
In the sea of mirth
To the point of gifting it

When I am alone

quite oft when I am alone
and alone is my eternal condition
I come to think of nothing
but thoughts that strangle
in the room where someone bid the world farewell
I come to think how burdened and how ardent I
am for a talk, a small talk that would spread its wings
and clear my thoughts
a talk that has no ending, always in crescendo
the surroundings would complain
I talk much
I confabulate stories more than the usual
only to kill the hissing silence
quite oft when I am alone
I yearn for the sound of steps
that walk by

I listen, as it were a prayer that purges
and I pray that someone opens the damned door
only to talk
for hours or days
sometimes the steps obey and come
but much of the time they coldly ignore
only to leave me lonelier, as I decay in silence

M.J. Iuppa

No One Owns the Clouds

Lately, when I find myself outside,
and moving slowly, I watch my steps,
careful not to lose my footing in my

preoccupation, which makes me stop
to remember where I'm going, what
small task I need to finish before

coming back into the warmth of
the kitchen, the smells of Sunday
roast, the sounds of logs shifting

their weight in the wood stove.

I pause, knowing I
have lost my center, my point of
purpose, and I look up and see the

trees, naked and unnatural, in winter's
waning light—a silhouette that could
be a mirror reflection, an image of

poverty that's nearly invisible, only
I'll see it deeply, with so many clouds
moving into a stillness— waiting

to comfort me.

First published in Third Wednesday (print edition) March 2020

G. Murray Thomas

Ed Jamieson

Cardboard Condominium

A cardboard dwelling
held together with rotten wood
leans against a pillar
under a freeway overpass.
It's a two room deluxe with no bathroom,
but with plenty of backyard.
¬gravel dirt floor is covered
with old blankets and clothes.
The cracks in the wood are the windows;
the scenery is concrete and asphalt.
The door is for crawling in and out,
there is no welcome mat.
The exhaust from the cars and the garbage fumes
keep unwanted visitors away.
No kitchen, no telephone, no cable t.v.,
no air conditioning for the hot summer nights,
no heat for the cold winter nights,
but the rent is free.

Frank Kearns

Coffee Cup Rosary

after Juan Felipe Herrera

Our Father who sat in silence
hallowed be thy thoughts,
thy troubled times,
thy meditations,
that haunt those who go on without you.
Give us this day thy spirit,
as we face our doubts and transgressions,
filter them through thy coffee and smoke,
let us find the strength you found,
in the dark of the early morning,
Amen.

Robert Keeler

The Cloud Appreciation Society

Clouds, mainly gray or white, nothing but wet
wind and frilly metaphors; they present
random shapes—like Rorschach tests
to probe our id—then slide away
to conspire.

Weighing tons not ounces, enjoying neither
spine nor inner strength, nor brains nor hearts;
sophisticated, meek—clouds never take orders.
Rogue cabals guide them, push them across outer
worlds, into boiling Venuses.

Clouds innocently look to dive underground
but resurface out of hot springs or lava cones,
or take on tormented, snake-like, and zebra shapes.

May I be allowed to live in my own cloud forever
until my waters boil away, then, make my way
out beyond Saturn's unmanageable rings,

or start over at home as a copper tea kettle
with no painful attachments, or live
in some damp mist, never needing parlors

full of goshawks
and caterpillars, their cocoons
unraveling into wisps.

Lalo Kikiriki

Comfort and Joy

I sleep in this desert of dreams
a place
where odd things happen

under the rocky pedernal
wakened
by dusk-neon sky

someone had left a bottle of
that sweet
old Southern Comfort

in a high cupboard, abandoned
for years
forgotten, perhaps...

Everyone thinks, "Janis Joplin"-
we do,
who have heard her story.

From a dead man's souvenir glass
I drink
three shots in a row,

pausing after each for a breath...

Alice
would know: wait for it.

Three kisses and honey warming
my heart
and on to the blood

through a back door to the
cosmos
Janis
would know: look up!

Under the Milky Way tonight
oh, yes
poems drop like stars

Two by Diane Klammer

love, love

For Susan K. Mack
"Like when I close my eyes, and don't even care if anyone sees me dancing."
Ben Rector Brand New

1
The ball is in your court, in the muted evening, the safe
netted place where you and I go to return the ball to each other,
with measured moments, graceful technique, like two dancers.

love love.

That's how the game starts,
can quickly turn into a contest for points.
We can bat this chartreuse orb around all night, not noticing the cyclic moon at all.
Then we start keeping score, which may lead to conflict.
It is better to keep score counting backwards.
I'd rather do a rally where we play in tandem without stopping.

But to make progress, we must remember the rules of the game as they were written.
Maybe love love meant something back when we were kids, and we forgot what it was.
Sometimes we must compensate and be two people at once.
One to cover front and one in the back,
to cover the entire court as if we could create distance
with more of the same.
Balls bounce back and forth and echo in our ears,
along with thwack of the tennis rackets.

2

A woman must wear many hats, bracelets,
tennis shoes to keep up with the game.
And those balls come with such velocity.
Hopscotch to it. Run.
Toss back the work.
Volley the family, the labor, the lousy healthcare.
Slam the third shift of makeup and clothes.
Return the rent, the mortgage payments.

Each one of these jobs is returned to its own part of the court.
She must keep her eyes on all the balls
as they rush at her.
Sometimes she wants to leave them all behind and go elsewhere.

But after the game of tennis gets going,
and it can be a smooth rally,
as there is a meditative quality, a simplicity
about the rhythm, repetition, work, movement, pathos,
the camaraderie of friendship, given and returned.

3

What is going to happen after the game?
Who will be bringing us home?
Can I think you into existence,
if we reside both within and outside this game?

The streets are dark and the moon has been waning for weeks,
trying to ignite itself back to clarity, sending its threads of light down to the players.   > > >

>>> So, the rallies go on
back and forth, serve and return.
During the rain and the snow,
people still show up to play them.

The neon colored balls remind me of a harvest moon
That shines down on the court for weeks,
that has forgotten to wax or wane,
but just stays there lighting its weary beacon on the game.
And no one notices its static nature.
But it's not so bad to be stuck under a stationary moon.
Better than no moon at all.

But what happens after the harvest is over?
Do we just go back to being who we were if we can even remember who that was?
Worry can swell like a solid moon into the minds of us both.
Meanwhile, are we just batting balls to each other,
waiting for meaningful life to continue?
The journey between two players takes a lifetime to develop.

Tennis can lead to something more,
friendly and competitive, gaming together.
Something real, lest we forget reality,
truth taking its turns with story.

The game of tennis may go on for years,
with partners meeting each other
throughout all kinds of circumstances.
The mazes we push ourselves through and beyond,
are just those…….mazes and games.

In the final analysis, I think only the love is real.

Who Wrote This Reality, Black Mirror?

"Out, damn spot." William Shakespeare

The great paradox has descended.
What saves you can kill you.
Social spacing is mandatory for safety.

The human presence that helps elevate
and validate each other with comfort,
now told to distance, to flatten the curve.

The human smile that could save, masked,
that reassured during most natural crises,
hands that touch, react to you, gloved,

now potentially deadly, have been transformed.
People have become walking germ incubators
and must be avoided, not embraced.

I have taken to singing reassurance on the bike trails,
under my headphones to communicate a message,
a living connection in six feet of separation, auditory flower.

Food shopping, necessity shopping
has become so weird, a perpetual sunset.
People wander in stores looking like aliens.

"Am I in a Twilight Zone military hospital?
No, this is the grocery store, ten at a time,
in line where we come for our daily bread."

You must trust the one
who cuts up, prepares your
Cobb Salad, puts it in the box.

The COVID Virus can live on metal,
live on cardboard, can freeze.
Wash your soda and beer cans.

Throw away outer wrappers.
Turn your kitchen counter into
a germ reduced surgery table

with strong disinfectant wipes.
Create two sides, one for the dirty,
one for clean, for food to be stored safely.

Wash produce like hands, for twenty seconds.
What does one needs for a good appetite?
The apple that sustains us shines double sided.

Doug Knott

Apology to Greta Thunberg

How about that Climate Change?

You're right, kid!
We spent it, we drove it,
we burned it, we fueled it
We bought it, we rode it,
But we didn't pay for it –
Didn't know it was your future, too -

We are your distinguished elders
And came of age just before the peak of the wave,
and we've surfed it to the shore, rolling in like pearls.
We're the coolest, we didn't even work for it,
it just got laid on us by the big living earth Gaia -
"Yes" - she said, "take my breast"
and we took her blood, skin and bones, too.

And our generation has enjoyed every possibility of living
whatever we want, wherever we choose to go.
We are the party of freedom - meaning
we partied with freedom

Now we're those hard-boiled eggs in the sunset.
What do you want from us?
Please deliver your rage to our chattering class,
We are the tribe - the human tribe –
And we welcome you to this fat-ball planet
Where we're all born out of God's Word

And when we get hungry
We go out on the crinkle-bulgy landscape
and kill kill kill a big elephant to feed our tribe.
Lots of meat meat meat we eat eat eat
Then dance pray fuck – then pray fuck dance
Afterwards, sleepity-sleep.

Then... get up, have coffee -- and make civilization! –
hammocks, clay pots, sexy figurines of gods,
Broadway plays - we create a world of light and dark
Sex, poetry, ocean-going plastic, capitalism, terrorism, religion

A house fantastic for us alone!
O throw open the green shutters of the world, and
make it brown and naked.

Enough – We hungry again!
Let's get another elephant --
Or at least an In-and-Out Burger
There's always more food, isn't there?

It will all work out ...(somehow)
There will be a solution ...(somehow)
But somehow, all that gets fuzzy when I try to think about it.
I can't shoot that hoop of what to do

You say the only way is massive political action?
No oil, and don't eat nothing in plastic?
Not a chance, even if everyone else does it!
Who helps who control who?

The earth is so stressed digesting us
Where can it shit, except on you?
So sorry, we knew, but didn't know
and now you know, but what to do?

Also there is no individual guilt,
We're all absolved and complicit.
All I ever did was drive my car and turn on
the house-lights and some air-con --
Me such a tiny, ordinary consumer!

In case the planet might shrug us off
You might consider the intrinsic death-wish of the species.
And all that plastic in the guts of whales?
We share the gifts.

Climate change is a spiritual vaccination
For those of us on the edge of the afterlife.
The seas will rise, the continents fall

I thought I'd never live to see it happen,
But I was wrong.

Jacqueline Kras

February 2019

You cannot give the words back to the nurses
This vocabulary you don't want is yours now
Technical medical terms with too many syllables
Make a repetition list you obsess over
The Words are your worry beads
Cold, passing through your fingers while you wait

If she was awake she'd joke about
How smart you'll sound at parties, all your fancy big Words to toss at drunk strangers
But she is uncharacteristically quiet
And notably far away

You start making a joke bank for later
Because there has to be a later
And her laughter in your life is non-negotiable

You get as close as you can without disrupting the wires and tubes
She wouldn't get mad about the snot you got on her gown
Or the tears or the kisses you placed in her hair
She would let it go
That you couldn't figure out what she tried to say
On day two
Around a breathing tube

She would also understand
Why you were terrified
That one time you came to visit
Because she rested peacefully
Instead of flinching and fighting

The machines are her functions
You love them and you want fewer of them
They blink and beep in simple alerts you would never have found alarming before
When anyone tries to say their noises are normal
You fail at masking your disbelief

Jacquline Kras

Everyone is doing their best
Everyone
You know well enough how sometimes people say that
With a sense of pity or dismissal
Forgiveness and judgment built into it equally
You know certainly how it gets used as an excuse or a fuck you
But really
No one knows how to be this afraid
It is grief before loss and consuming uncertainty
Everyone is doing their best

Waiting is the only practice
Waiting is faith
Waiting is your marathon
Waiting is the channel and it's
all there is to tune to
(waiting is your heart rate)
Waiting is the one and only awful
loving hopeful thing to do.

Lucille Av

A virtuous street, lawns clipped and tidy. A virtuous street, its signage a caution to neighbors and strangers, its trees pruned and well-watered.

No body sleeps on a sidewalk. No graffiti slurs the masonry. No root shatters the pavement.

Houselots are small. Mortgages conform. Cars are legally parked.

At one end of the street, an all-way stop slows traffic to a residential pace.

At the other end, a church.

Outsiders never see Lucille. They're here for the beachfront. They never get out this far east.

And Lucille will never go west to meet them. The avenue stays put, hoarding its facts behind privacy fences.

On some streets, this isn't a city.

Mishkon and St. Marks

1.

Mishkon Tephilo is a synagogue at Main and Navy. Today, on Simchah Torah, Rabbi Botnick unbinds the Torah scroll. Eighty thousand words unspool along fifteen social hall tabletops, butt-ended one to the next.

The congregation recites the Torah's last verse. The law having been given, the story is done.

Now the scroll's axis reverses direction, rewinding the Word of God until only the first verses are visible.

Every year, for the first time again, heaven and earth are made anew.

2.

Two miles away at St. Marks, congregants kneel. At the rail, mouths await their redemption,
blind tongues suspended between estrangement and reconciliation.

The Body of Christ, says Father Spellman.

Amen, say the tongues.

Again and again, the Holy Spirit. Again and again, God on the tongue.

3.

Not many neighbors have ever heard of Mishkon or St. Marks. Why should they? In their
bedrooms they have built shrines to their own prophet of the eternal return. Tonight, in
each of these bedrooms, the prophet speaks:

> *Tomorrow along the coast*
>
> *expect early morning clouds*
>
> *burning off at noon*
>
> *leaving hazy sunshine*
>
> *& highs*
>
> *in the mid to upper 70s.*

Michou Landon

EverNoir

Black desert scarab--
Stink beetle--
Staggers in jagged circles
Across the desert mosaic…
Dense little licorice tank,
He is too black for this place,
Cannot blend anywhere,
And rambles as if from the exhaustion
of not belonging.

Yet the Raven, too, is Black--
So black he turns blue.
He carries his belonging with him, inside him,
In the *Wh!Wh!Wh!Wh!* of his wings,
Which sweep away all question of belonging,
And he lands with full (and comical) entitlement
Upon the cedar branch too limp to bear his weight,
And yet it does,
Through his sheer will to belong.

Donna Langevin

My Hands

miss how they used to grab
handrails on streetcars and buses,
trail fingers along counters,
cup palms around doorknobs.

They long for handshakes, high-fives,
petting a stranger's dog
instead of stroking my fake-fur blanket.

My hands miss picking my nose and teeth
and letting me suck their digits.

My hands wish they were naked
with someone else, also naked.

My hands worry they are shrinking
to baby-size with atrophied string-like fingers.

They become autumn leaves
about to fall from my wrists.

Lonely as fish, without a lake to swim in,
their river-veins flow nowhere now
and their rivulet-lines
long to be signs or love letters.

My hands miss reaching out
without synthetic skins.

Fingers intertwined,
they now clasp each other like kin.

inspired by Ballad of a Hand, by Jon Lajoie

Three by Laura Munoz-Larbig

Protest Déjà Vu

Activists are in the streets again. It is a déjà vu of protests against a new establishment.

Not just adults march in protest now; not just college students angry with government policies.

Now, teens still in high school join the march, led by the youngest who have the most to dread.

These children have endured school deaths and fear a future with a poisoned earth. The kids are angry.

They march against all that we protested back in the '60s, and more. Establishment claws have dug deeper, enslaving our lives.

In the last century, we sought freedom and peace; in this millennium, we found impoverishment as incomes fell below living needs.

We failed even as we won wars. We lost the fight to be free from poverty and homelessness.

The world's youths have noticed:
The dreams of the 60s have died. Changes promised were lies. So the world's angry teens have taken up the old dreams.

I wonder, if these fierce youths fail, will we all lose the way to freedom's trail?

GIVE ME LIBERTY OR

GIVE ME DEATH!!

Raindog

Rain Lullaby

Wrapped up in a blanket like a cocoon, I push back the driver's seat and lie down to sleep.

It is cold outside. Surprisingly, it is warm inside.

The wind howls against the windows. The sky restlessly rumbles as rain softly dances a pitter-patter pattern upon the car's roof.

The rhythm becomes a sonata that lulls me to sleep. In my hidden car, a rain lullaby drifts me away to dream under a homeless sky.

Under the Crescent Moon

Beneath a darkening clear blue New Year's eve, we huddle in the light of one diamond star shining near the year's first waxing crescent moon. Libations of beer and vodka passes in a circle from one homeless hand to another.

In a few more months, the ninth month of their calendar, Muslims will celebrate Ramadan, when the crescent moon and star arise together, signaling the time for rituals of abstinence and austerities.

This January, we homeless celebrate nothing but our friendships forged by our homelessness. Our ritual is passing around bottles of alcohol in a circle.

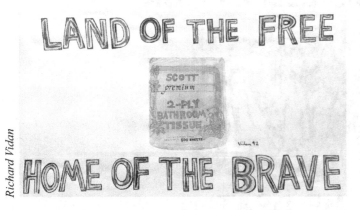

I look up to admire the celestial beauty above, surrounded by the friendship of homeless souls below.

For us, our spiritual cleansing are not brought on by yearly rituals of crescent moons and stars; they are a constant ritual of stoic lives due to poverty, with austerities imposed upon us by our homelessness.

Kyle Laws

Two Women With Cat

My sister reminds me about the cat
that we took to the New Jersey suburb
of Philadelphia, who didn't want to live there
and traveled 75 miles back to the house on the bay.

We found her in the spring when we returned
to open up the house, turn on the water drained.
She had lived the winter in the cellar.
After months in the suburb, I agreed with her choice.

She had tangled with another animal, survived.
Her throat was torn and she could hardly speak.
What I imagine a woman in a burqa feels,
what an artist senses trying to paint women sheltered

when we would prefer chance to security,
prefer a life lived to safety, prefer to be a black cat
scorned and left behind to fend on its own,
prefer the sliver of a crescent moon to a full at epigee.

Previously published in Ekphrastic Review

Marie C. Lecrivain

Why David Carradine
Was a Karmic Masochist

You can first spot it
in the film Boxcar Bertha;
that moment, as Union Bob,
when he's crucified
to the door of the train,
his piercing screams
bordered on ecstasy.

In every episode of Kung Fu,
he's tied up (and down),
put in cuffs and chains,
and hung from the rafters
like a Thanksgiving turkey
in a farmer's barn.

It was in the way
he held himself close,
like a wonderful, terrible secret.

It was written in the marks
on his neck when police found
him bound to a travel hanger
in a hotel closet, his pupils
black, blind, and stilled
from the final satiation
la grande mort brings.

Previously published in
Rat's Ass Review, © 2019

John B. Lee

Sometimes when a man...

sometimes when a man
builds himself a nest
in a ravine
at the water's edge
the comparison
to an oriole's woven home
or a squirrel's
tattered domain as seen
in the high scatter of a denuded
late-autumn oak
fixed there in the precarious gravity
of thin branches
along with the last rag scraps of lazy weather
or perhaps
the simile of wasp hives in winter
their mud-and-paper domicile abandoned
in the black-mood cold
of November

sometimes that analogy breaks down
when the heart tumbles into poverty
and despair for
someone's hopeless with the drink
or someone's lost to the needle
and the cruel oblivion
of freebase and a burning match
or the locked up madness of a closed village
but there
in the thought hollow of this common trail
in that low copse
by the reed bed of a slow stream
someone has built themselves
a shelter

and this particular architect
has talent as with the expertise
of a bent-branch sanctuary
crafted like a birch bark house
the open door to the south
the windward rise parqueted with dry stone
the floor made from
four old boards rotten wet on the bottom
keeping the damp at bay for the body of the sleeper
and a blue tarpaulin
tethered to the four winds
to keep out the rain

this son of Adam
has foraged for a full white bucket
of firewood
and though he is not there
he keeps his story
in the lonesome file
he keeps his life in the star chamber
where the lost fire goes

and the oriole - oh - he is beautiful and gone
and the squirrel is busy teaching the branch
to hold him leaping
and the wasp is wintering in the wall
when the world we dream
comes howling
with the wolf's knowledge
of moonlight
and the coyote who shares his name with heaven

Two by Rick Leddy

Window

I look out the hospital window and I see
Shimmering, swaying palm trees brushed by afternoon light
Silent movie movement below
All the lives intermingling
Rushing from here to there
Intersecting, bisecting
It is so lovely and yet so ordinary
I want to cry from the sheer miracle of it
Each shadow, every step, the subtle motion of life around us
The beauty of it almost too much to bear

Rivulets of sorrow run wet down my cheek
On this side
The gravity of the world thick and heavy
In this world of machines and hushed tones
Friends gathered
In a room filled with waiting
And ending

I look out the window
Sitting among rows of empty chairs
Filled with ghosts of grief
And I sense you
On the other side
You will always be there
Nestled in dappled light and gentle breezes
The sunlight filtering through your dreams
Memories of you alighting in empty spaces

I look out the window,
through the thin, transparent barrier between
Here and There
Birth and Death   > > >

> > > Beginnings and Endings
Love and Loss
The horizon outstretched and hazy
A million miles and just a grasp away
Inching toward us all
I watch the hurrying lives below
Seeking destination
And I know you have found yours
You reside in the waking dawn and fiery sunset
Between the beats of our broken hearts
Filling the void between falling tears
You rest in the quiet moments behind closed eyes
Your home is within us

I look out the window
And I see you
Knowing
You will always be there
Revealing yourself in the symphony of the every day

The random gesture
A beautiful brush stroke
The laughter of a stranger
Reminding us of you
A thousand memories
Floating
Ready to attach themselves to us

I look out the window
Life swimming in blurred sunlight
My eyes filled with wet memories
Inhaling the joy of a beautiful life
And exhaling the sharp grief of loss

Feeling
So lucky
So Grateful
To have been your friend

Rick Leddy

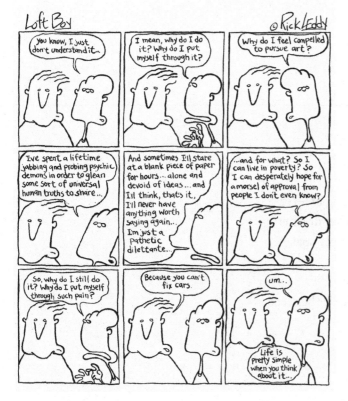

Venn Diagrams

I order a Tourette's stutter of a beer
and wonder what others think
As they casually toss youth and naïveté
Into the false dusk
An old man sitting alone, reading
Loser, Loner, Malcontent, Poet
Bleeding dreams that flow and dissipate into the banter
I watch the beer glass sweating circles on a white paper napkin
Dark jagged fingers dissolving, expanding, forming Venn Diagrams
I remember bright, retro coasters
Colorful solid squares with neat graphics,
Thick vanguards against the permanence of casual and thoughtless stain
I can't remember exactly when the coasters vanished,
When they were replaced by casual neglect
Left to be eaten away
by the wet cancer of each new round

I try to recall when it was that everything
became nothing except the squatter that lives deep inside
This uninvited sadness that can't be evicted
At least I'll never drink alone, I think
A sharp ice storm of a joke
The laughter trapped thick and glacial in my chest

Nobody knew my name
When I walked in
And nobody will when I leave
As I watch my dark circles grow
Attempting to form Venn diagrams
that will never intersect

Two by Linda Lerner

A cover-up

when a large horse stumbled
in Central Park and collapsed,
news spread of his inhumane treatment
to all of us, stumbling in uncertainty;
no way to explain what couldn't happen
is happening; political weather
grew more turbulent, warnings
about everything descended

and when I just about had enough
fever and a hacking cough put a stop
to it; for three weeks I was inoculated,
nothing could touch me.

Until that horse. Feeling better
meant I could smell him now
this horse I never even saw, learned
had shown signs of distress
before collapsing, a struggle to cover up
put him out of the way fast
keep people from seeing:
what we feared afterwards
had nothing to do with a horse.
And couldn't be euthanized so easily.

This War / That War

A Nam Vet once told me that soldiers
fooled by cute hungry children
used as suicide bombers
they'd reach out to with candy

became victims too, like us now, those
we live and work with, our neighbors
who don't know what toxic substance
they're carrying, endangering
their own lives and ours

people we need the most
sought comfort with in cafes
and restaurants after 9/11,
forbidden now. We crouch

In makeshift fox holes six feet apart
in cities across America, watch
each other, listening for a cough
the ticking time bomb
we rush home to defuse

Raindog

Two by Jane Lipman

Song of the Unemployed Buddhist

I work at a switchboard—connected
        and disconnected
    at once.

I plugged the wrong lawyer's mother
    into the wrong
    senior law partner—

as you've guessed, I'm no longer
    connected.

    Being fired—
        one of the discontinuous risings
    and fallings
    in the parade of thoughts, feelings,
        experiences

        in the ever-changing display
    of impressions, actions, sensations

        in the vast, open
    field of awareness

        where doorways go both ways—
    into the rising and falling
    or into the infinite.

But law partners, Cutter, Ouster, and Ritter
    don't understand anything of Buddhism
    or see beyond their $1500 Armani mirror shades.

They take workshops on how to rid themselves of guilt
    for charging over $350 per hour.

And me? I have to admit, I'd like to stuff them
        with oily tomatoes and punt them to Syria.
        But if I go down that avenue

they'd probably become refugees, tragic boat people,
        arrive in my town, melt my heart,
        and I'd take them in.

So I may as well take the short cut,
        do my Buddhist practice: enfold them,
        and my own anger and intolerance of them

in gentleness, let it percolate, soften
        and open my heart. Relax
        into the vast awareness
        that contains it all.

But they *do* have a mother problem!

Gentleness answers: You're right.
Now hush.
Die to who you thought you were.
Die to who you thought they were.
Die.
Die.

Songbird Coming out of Ash

An encounter with Death is an encounter with the Self.
––Carl Jung

One morning I'm at your grave
trying to dig you up.
Crazy. Traci-comedic.
My bare hands
don't get far…strew instead
the carton of strawberries over your grave…
Miriam Makeba's "Love Tastes
Like Strawberries"—a song I then loved.

Dream: You are standing in Monticello Road,
the steep hill a gushing river of gasoline.
Your wrists are tied; you are
ankle-deep in gasoline trying to light a match.

I, too, was a time bomb ticking for one to five years
after you took your life.
Spinning in memories, I get up from the computer.
Do I want to go back into all that?

Hours in reverie, witnessing the movie
of that part of our lives…the old
haunts, dramas, scenes…
what Papaji called: sucking bones
in the graveyard, drinking
your own blood.

A new character, Awareness
Aware of Itself, enters:
accompanies me. At your grave
(and mine, in a way) it picks me up, carries me out
of there. Carries me far away
to here   and now.

There have been choice points.
The blood-curdling, freeing scream
that came out of me (involuntary,
but still a choice)…when I asked Mother

for the third time how you died,
and got told that night: I'm too tired.

The next morning: Later. All the people
are arriving. Last, a double message from Dad
pulled out my scream. Mother hollered,
You're not going to any funeral––
(like it was a party). When I saw
the cars parked behind mine, unintentionally
blocking me from leaving, I chose
to call a cab. I had to see you,
or would never believe it had happened,
Mother yelling dramatically as I left:
Now you'll have to know what I know.

At the funeral parlor, the director asked,
Do you know how he died? I stared at him helpless,
praying for the grace of an answer.
He quietly said, A fall from height.
God bless strangers who will answer
burning questions   with truth.

The rest, my precious,
our visit, and your visitation,
you know.

No, I don't choose to write all that again.
Drama lurks, storm-like, always at the periphery.

My ego loves that stuff.
My essence doesn't.

Recently, sleepless one night, I got entangled,
like a dolphin in seaweed and fishermen's nets,
in a stupid catch 22 interior drama I still don't see how
I could have resolved differently. Decided, for me,
it's unsolvable, a waste of precious life…and left it.
Should it surface again, that's what to do,
leave, turn off the juice.

Revelation!—— Freedom, like happiness, can be a
choice!

What I lost when Barry died, was a soulmate.
What I retrieved and kept is my own soul.

*

When danger approaches, sing to it.
——Arab Proverb

All is God…the four deer daily, nightly,
coming to the garden, drinking up the birdbath,
nibbling new green nourishing growth…holy
mountain,
holy mountain bluebird, holy coronavirus,
holy homemade masks, holy toilet paper,
holy wipes, holy laughter, holy struggle,
holy defeat,
holy Derek, my neighbor, who died alone/not alone,
his dog Cedric was with him; holy Jason, his friend
and co-worker who broke a window and found him;

holy Jason listened to Derek's phone messages,
including mine and phoned me; holy Bill, their
employer,
who told me everything he knew——unknown by
anyone but him,
Derek had two forms of cancer; my holy friends
who said prayers with me over phones;
holy Debbi giving this class, asking holy
questions:
what did you lose and what did you keep?
giving me and others a holy chance
to write through holy grief again…or not;
holy long roots of white hair coming through the
red,
holy wind, holy sun, holy pinecone, holy New
York friend
mailing me three holy masks made in Japan
as I mail her holy nitrile gloves, blue;
holy Ruth mourning Derek and Cedric,
holy hug we shared yesterday, weeping,
holy disobeying covid-19's holy restrictions,
holy choice, holy loss, holy heartbreak, holy love.

Ellaraine Lockie

Nominative Determinism
--A found poem*

1. trump as verb: beat, break, checkmate, concoct, cook up, conceive, create, crush, contrive, defeat, devise, distort, dominate, drub, excel, edge, fabricate, frame, fake, get the better of, get the upper hand, hatch, invent, make up, nose out, outfox, outdo, outmaneuver, overtake, outperform, outstrip, outwit, overcome, overpower, prevail, profit, scheme, surpass, top, trounce, vanquish, wallop, win

2. trumpery as noun: babble, balderdash, bits and pieces, blah, blather, bullshit, bunk, bunkum, castaways, castoffs, chaff, claptrap, cultch, debris, detritus, discards, dominance, dreck, drivel, drool, falderal, foam, foolishness, froth, fudge, funk, garbage, gobbledegook, gibberish, hogwash, horsefeathers, humbug, idiocy, Jabberwocky, jargon, jive, litter, leverage, malarkey, nonsense, odds and ends, poppycock, raff, refuse, rejects, remnants, riffraff, rubbish, rubble, swill, tatters, trash, trickery, tommyrot, twaddle, waste material, wealth, wreckage

3. trumpery as adjective: base, beggarly, brummagem, cheap, commonplace, flashy, foolish, gaudy, garish, inferior, insignificant, immaterial, little, mean, mediocre, meretricious, nasty, obscene, ostentatious, puny, pretentious, poor, rubbishy, schlock, scrubby, second-rate, shabby, shoddy, showy, slight, small, tawdry, trashy, trifling, trivial, two-bit, twopenny, unimportant, valueless, vulgar, worrisome, worthless, worst, wretched

Raindog

4. trump up: color, conceal, disguise, falsity, garble, gloss over, hide, mislead, misstate, misrepresent, pervert, twist, warp

5. trump card: ace in the hole, card up one's sleeve, leg up, secret advantage, secret weapon, upper hand, whip hand

*Collected from selected thesauri

Nominative determinism: the hypothesis that people tend to gravitate towards areas of work that fit their name

Radomir Vojtech Luza

Beautiful Disaster

In the sea slug of my mind
The beach would be snow white
Cars move like bullets

Freeways made of cotton candy
Not blood

In this tepid tundra
This inebriated concoction of a town

I stand put
And say yes

Your Sunset Boulevard beaded costume
Jim Morrison improvised headache

Peppering their way
Into my heart

Your non-embraceable children
Bi-polar bankruptcies

Blue sky suicides
Valley gang scene
Are skin

Your incredible, deplorable
Joyous jam box

Of a roller coaster ride
Becoming less bumpy

Your Jesus Jews
Transgender tambourines

Leave me afraid
Yet seeking more

I want more than just
To grow accustomed

To your tender temper tantrums
Worn weather wilderness

I want to love you

INTERVIEW

SANTA FE POET
BASIA MILLER

Interview by RD Armstrong

BASIA MILLER'S bio reads like an academic fairy tale. She grew up on a farm in Manhattan, KS. where she graduated from High School in 1954. Off to Antioch College in Ohio, where she received a B.A. in Philosophy. She became a member of Antioch Abroad, an exchange program with a French family (in her case). During the summer she worked on their farm, where she learned to speak French. In the fall she attended the University of Besancon.

In 1962, she earned her M.A. at the University of Chicago, in the Dept. of Romance Languages, but didn't get her P.H.D. Until 1989, she worked on a team that translated Montesquieu into modern English. She taught in the University of Chicago's Basic Program of Liberal Education from 1981 – 88. In 1988 she joined the faculty of St. John's College, Santa Fe, NM.

Later during her sabbatical year, 1996 – 97, in France she met a couple whose life was dedicated to books and art. They hit it off and have been inviting her to join them in southern France the past 24 years. Because of this connection, Basia has made a real "French connection" with the French poets of the area. It's been a remarkable life!

RD: *You mention in your bio that "intuition is at the heart of creativity." Could you elaborate on that?*

B: Thanks for that question, RD. It's interesting to ask if intuition can enrich creativity. Sometimes, while I'm writing, I look at a developing poem and ask if I'm molding it according to some pre-set idea of genre, form, or logic. I like to test my writing in process, to see if I can give rein to some of my wilder impulses. This is a fascinating thing to explore, but it doesn't originate with me. I belong to a group of poets and artists based in Paris called the Intuitists. Eric Sivry and Sylvie Biriouk, the founders, propose that intuition is at play where you find discontinuity, uncertainty, unpredictable collisions, and the like. The idea is roughly that if intuition is active at the very moment of creation, it frees the writer or artist from a pre-existing order. At annual conferences I've given two papers on the role of intuition in translation. That sounds counterintuitive if you think that there is no latitude in translation, but I know it works in some translations as well as in my own poetry.

RD: *You have been an avid workshop participant since you retired from academia. I wonder if you could tell us about the transition from being a researcher of old poetry to a writer of your own, more modern, poetry?*

B: In a nutshell, being a teacher and translator for many years then suddenly, after retirement, recycling myself as a poet for the last ten was more a leap than a transition. I started out in the 60s teaching high-school French. I could feel the performance dimension of teaching even as I tried to mediate between text and students. It's necessary, but it doesn't lead me to the more private place of poetry. Later, as a translator of books from French to English, the work reinforced another habit, that of respecting well-defined and narrow limits. At that time, I thought words were either right or wrong.

I had spent a lot of time with French drama and poetry—from Racine to Verlaine, Rimbaud and Camus, but on looking back, I can sense that I rarely got past sounds and images to feelings, partly because I hadn't studied the language deeply enough.

Ten years ago, with my first poems, I could see I was shaping them according to a bookish mind-set that didn't leave space for the unexpected. All those wonderful workshop teachers helped me tap into my personal experiences. After a while some of the good things from my classic studies did come together with the poems, like train tracks merging in the distance. I began to use assonance, alliteration, metaphor, etc., with more discrimination.

RD: *I like what you wrote in your bio about "writing to gain insight and to amuse myself."*

What do you mean? The two goals seem unrelated, but are they?

B: There is something about words that is an invitation to play. I try all kinds of wording—I'm an perpetual, compulsive reviser—until something finally sounds better, sounds true. Maybe everyone has a private sense of what works that quietly guides the writing. I know that I write to invite readers to be willing to enter the experience that sounds true to me. Trying to write poems that are congruent with my private sense is a constant challenge. It requires me to keep my ear to the ground, I mean, my own ground, and not be seduced by other writers' wonderful poetry and lines of thought. Yes, for me gaining insight and amusing myself are related. I have a lot of conversations with myself about authenticity and I fret that I have a limited understanding of some of the topics I choose—like the roofers in my poem called « Ministers of Roofing »

Trump's 1ˢᵗ year in office. Documented. In real time.
How we got to where we are now.

- Poetry and prose describing the major events in our nation that set the path for America now.

- Winner of **6 national book awards,** including 3 first prize honors.

A BOOK FOR OUR TIMES!

Reading Tea Leaves After Trump

Thelma T. Reyna

Available now.

$14.95 + shipping
178 pages

Order at:
GoldenFoothillsPress.com
Amazon.com

that appeared in LUMMOX 8. I guess gaining insight and amusing myself have risk-taking in common.

RD: *I love New Mexico, especially Santa Fe and its many poets. What was it about this area that drew you to it? Is it the terrain or the people or..?*

B: I'm one of those lucky people who was invited to Santa Fe for a job. I taught at St. John's College, which was my dream-job, and I was there for 20 years. Coming from Chicago, I found that Santa Fe was quite a change—I didn't have to triple-lock my doors and I could just walk out and find the bowl of the blue sky above me.

RD: *This year looks to be a complete "washout" in terms of the things that most Americans like to do. Social distancing prevents most poets from doing what they like to do.... going out to hear and share with their comrades at poetry readings, poetry workshops, AA meetings etc. How does this self isolation affect you?*

B: Thank you for asking. I'm safe and healthy and in touch with friends. I do miss the open mics and reading groups, but so far the isolation has given me a fruitful time for reflection. You have to keep things in perspective. It breaks my heart every day to know that people are risking their lives for us —health-care, food, education, transportation, safety, journalism. On and on. Our lives are in their hands, but they're often not well paid and their work is not acknowledged nearly enough. The values in our country are topsy-turvy. So many people are in desperate situations. The pandemic is shining a bright light on that.

RD: *Did your association with the couple you met in France in 96-97 inspire you to learn*

more about expressing yourself poetically? If so, how?

B: How interesting that you relate my friends Marie and Pierre Cayol to my writing life. Marie, a writer and Pierre, a painter and print maker, have visited the Southwest nearly every year since 1981. They come for the summer to write, paint and support their friends in the Native American communities. For me, it was life-changing to get acquainted with people whose lives are devoted to creative work. It made me aware of how narrowly my energy was channeled into degrees and institutions rather than self-expression and art. Because they welcomed me, I became a member of quite a different community.

In 2008, they introduced me to a French poet, Francine Caron, who needed an English translator for her « Cantata for the Grand Canyon. » Over the next decade, we published that and other long poems together. (N.B. We communicated by snail mail because she doesn't use email.) This work has taken me to poetry

Raindog

Dearest Papa

A Memoir in Poems

National Award Winning Author
Thelma T. Reyna

"Beautifully crafted memoir poems....intimate, personal...."

"*A deep, detailed account of love....haunting and beautifully bold.*"

National award-winning Poet Laureate emerita Thelma T. Reyna depicts the brave, inspiring life and sudden death of her husband of 50 years, Victor, called Papa by those close to him. Book available now.

GoldenFoothillsPress.com
Amazon.com

$15 + shipping
116 pages

fairs and book launches in France. Knowing the Cayols and working with Francine gave me the confidence to self-publish my own poems and bring out a bilingual poetry book, The Next Village/Le prochain village, in 2016.

RD: *You have spent a lifetime understanding language in an academic setting, yet you were unmoved to 'jump into the pool', at least not until you retired. Was the wait worth it?*

B: Writing poetry has become so important to me. Now I have two communities--in France and Santa Fe--of generous artists, writers and poets--who are all in for the creative life. Frankly, I was probably not ready earlier to spend my time writing—I probably couldn't have imposed the structure on my life and the self-discipline that it requires. I've been terribly lucky in my life that things have turned up for me when I could most benefit from them.

RD: *How do you like your life now? What inspires you?*

B: I'm basically very satisfied with my life, though right now preoccupied with questions about how the world will look after the pandemic. Happiness means a lot to me. There were stretches—everyone has them--when I didn't see how it would turn out. I'm grateful to precious friends and family, therapy and a fair dose of innate optimism for the full life I have. What's been inspiring me in the last year or two is watching people work with their tools. Saul who comes to trim the gangly juniper in my front yard has an eye for its innate balance and uses his tools to bring that out. The Camassia Area in West Linn, Oregon, is maintained by volunteers whose work, while critically important, is almost invisible. This kind of result just thrills me. The beautiful world draws me out and I hope

I can participate in it for a good while yet.

RD: *Finally, you have been submitting to the LUMMOX Anthologies from the beginning; what do you think of LUMMOX Press's efforts to bring as broad a swath of poetry to readers as is possible?*

B: RD, because you recognize Game not Fame, LUMMOX Press offers something that's badly needed. The LUMMOX anthologies contribute a democratic model to a field that usually operates as a meritocracy. By publishing a rich and wide selection of poets and artists in the LUMMOX anthologies and awarding prizes and publication to prize-winners--not to mention interviews, essays, articles and reviews--you're supporting the People's creativity from the ground up. Bravo !

Educating Basia

I've wrangled Basia in the world for decades.
As a handle, she's slithery, hard to seize –
Spelling is tricky. She sounds foreign-made.
She escapes from her new friends' memories.

She needs to be tamed, with boundaries set for her
She needs to improve her relationship style
While she looks so special no one can ignore her,
she appears everywhere with a complex profile

She's Basha in Polish—it's short for Barbara,
that's her name in the family when they're at home
In Greece, the non-Greek is a « barbarian, »
not someone you'd ever want to have known.

She's Jewish. She contains divine goodnesses
as a daughter of God…that's the « bat » of bat-mitzvah.
She speaks Latin. The « Basia » of Catullus are « Kisses »
A thousand of them, the bouquet, is basia mille.

Eclectic, electric, Basia's been a live wire !
But if I give her strong models -- of a warm grip,
a simple door-handle, and a rug by the fire--
she'll slide on a handshake into easy friendship.

ANGELA CONSOLO MANKIEWICZ
POETRY CONTEST WINNERS

THIS YEAR'S JUDGE: B.J. BUCKLEY

WHAT THE JUDGE, B.J. BUCKLEY, HAD TO SAY ABOUT THIS YEAR'S CONTEST...

The work submitted to this contest was a truly amazing group of poems. I've judged a number of such competitions over the years, and most times only a few truly shine out. Not so here; the variety of form and subject matter, as well as the attention to voice and craft by every single author made it very very difficult to winnow. The titles throughout especially pleased me. That seems a small thing, but too many writers of poetry toss them off, when a title should be the hand extended from writer to reader which leads them into the poem. The works I selected kept rising to the top through multiple readings of the entire group, and for each one, though in different ways, the title grabbed me and pulled me in, and then the poem wouldn't let me go. The overall quality of the submissions restores my faith in the daily importance of poetry in America as a vital mode of communication. All of these folks got GAME in capital letters.

FIRST PLACE

John B. Lee
Pt. Dover, ON

When Love is Like Knocking the Clay from the Plough

in the silage
and on the hay
in the fragrance of
rolled oats and molasses
and as it is
with the sweet odour
of cut grass and cow flap still green
or the high pong
of hog chop or how
wheat straw smells of mid-summer sunlight
softening the mow
or dust in the bean row
with dirt choking the light
as it dims with the tilth of the day
turning the earth
on the spring tooth and the harrow
or under the giant drum
of the roller
a rock-rattle watched for leveling
so the wind-wild soil   > > >

>>> will settle upon the sewn seed
all these and a closing in of white
on the bird-limed stone
oat chaff and marrow
and swine spoor
flung at the root and draping the fences
in timothy strings
dripping the redolent rags of manure
a dark wake
a wide swath
a visceral moment of darkness come shallow
in shades like shadows in trees
that follow the man in the field
first catching blue air
and then falling
transforming the mutable glebe
with fertile aromas
ammonium rich and …
reminding how love is
like knocking the clay from the plough
or what
flies from the tread of the wheel
when the tractor comes home in the dark

whenever I feel
the heart in the heat of a thigh
next to mine
or a palm warm as a pulse
on the back of my hand
I am there in the youth
of first things
made memory deep
as the full boat
rides deep and so deeper for that
in the come-to-me cresting of waves

Elevator Girl

it's hard to resist
making a salacious joke
about the lifelong occupation
of the woman
who for almost thirty-five years
operated the Otis-Fensom elevator
at Kingsmill's Dry Goods Store
on Dundas Street in London-ont
indeed, there's something
heroic to be said
of someone who
with the expertise of Phileas Fogg
could find level floating
with the floor lever
of the lift
easing it down
so the lips of the sill
met as though for a kiss
and so you might
glide without worry of tripping
and then
there were the brass
scissor doors to consider
and of course
the needfulness of bells
chiming the presence
of someone waiting somewhere
like a ghost imagining levitation

you'd make little boys
titter behind their hands

The Snake

to hear you utter the words Ladies Lingerie
as they tumbled out
the door delightfully informed
by mothers with naughty children
dragged beyond the hoistway
into the glamour
of mannequins in black brassiere
and of course
a director of blue movies
has made a film called Elevator Girl
about a nymphomaniac
who fantasized all day
behind a shy smile

but that wasn't you -- no
you wore sensible shoes
and a smart frock
fighting off ennui
behind your smile
making chit chat with shopping strangers

while only you knew how your husband
who waited at home
had been destroyed by the war
five years in a Stalag
starved on grass soup
under a sky
which even then
was sometimes shining and blue
as the best-fired China in Dresden

I hear the sibilant snake
essing into the grass below the stairs
quick as a lace you might pull from a boot
fast as the slipping of silk
from a nail
and though he or she
is benign, still I feel
a primordial shiver of natural fear
like the first frisson of desire
in the heel-bitten myths
of an innocent child
chasing the flames of Eden

what vanishes
like water in runnels
of rain after rain in cracked clay
or shadows made brilliant
by time-measured light
or a dream when you wake
to what's real in the room where you sleep
as you move out of darkness where darkness is truth
where the heart at rest
isn't blue though
it proves itself blue
where it blooms in your veins
and what darkness reveals
isn't red
though fire be red
where it touches the mind from within

oh little snake
I stand and watch you
where you go beyond watching
into occupied green of the weed-wild earth
the listening green of untameable earth

SECOND PLACE

Elaine Mintzer

Manhattan Beach, CA

In Orbit: A Sestina

How quickly the days go down
like sunny pills, never getting stuck
in the throat or triggering a reflex.
Dawn, dusk, or in prayer
to the eastern or western suns, around
we go though I stand, still

spinning 1,000 miles an hour, still
in my chair at my desk where up and down
are apparent if not true, and round
is irrelevant on the cosmic map. I'm stuck
with old reference points. No prayer
comes to my lips. I've squelched that reflex

for good. Yet the longing for heaven--that reflex--
remains here in my pocket. I remember still
the fruitless desire, the futile search. A prayer
in the well: a penny, a nickel, celestial body down
to the unseen mossy bottom, stuck
between two rocks that had surrendered to round,

sharp edges gone. Even so, round
does not remove danger. My reflex
is to ride the ellipse. How many times can I get stuck
in this cycle of worry? Day and night. Still
and wild. Every up with an exquisite down.
Even if I had one, I haven't got a prayer

of surviving. Three funerals this year. Another prayer
to comfort the living. Another round
at the buffet table -- potato salad, cold cuts, then down

the stairs where there's no place to sit. Only in reflex
the widow smiles, her empty eyes stuck
in polite horror. Focused still

on the one who could not make this party, the still
player beyond the game, beyond this prayer,
for the last time in these garments stuck,
wedged in the dark wish, becoming round
with the earth, one with the cycle of decay, the reflex
of microbial life breaking down.
the world to its smallest element, laying down
its last prayer to be absorbed by reflex
back into the cosmos, no longer still, spinning around.

In Tongues

Listen: what I want to say is I can't pray. I can't
put want into words. I won't
say words someone else has written. I'd rather
talk in tongues and string syllables into holy
glossolalia. I'd rather be a Quaker, silent
in my silent pew. A green-forest rambler
who finds peace beneath quaking boughs.
Or the sea-stone picker who stalks
the broken-shell shoreline, who quarrels
with gulls in my own shrill and broken cry.

Grafting

Maybe it starts with the kiss, a pressing
of self to self, an opening
of one to another down to heartwood, open
to the elements.

The arborist cuts a notch in the trunk, places
the new variety in the wound, binds
the two together until they share every
thing, confuse which is which,
who is who.

Whose leaf?
Whose limb?
Whose sun?

THIRD PLACE

Alexis Fancher

San Pedro, CA

Alexis Fancher

Poem For Kate In Chemo

Above where your right breast used to be the oncologist
implanted a port to make things easier. "It takes forever,"
you say. "An hour's drive, each way, an entire day used up,
laying there."

But first, the tourniquet, tied to your upper arm, the
cheery nurse, tapping for a working vein, your thick
blood at last flooding into one syringe after another.
Then the weigh-in, each time less. "Bone and skin
now," you say.

If your numbers are good, you head to the chemo
room, rows of cushy recliners, supplicants tethered
to plastic bags held high by IV poles, a forest of
metal trees.

You unbutton your blouse, offer up the convenient port
to a flush of saline - like ocean, you tell me, like waves.

Next, the chemicals, those shimmering droplets
riding the plastic tube into your chest,

a kind red blanket, thrown over
your legs.

I tear the best *New Yorker* short stories from the
magazine and mail them to you in Port Townsend.
Something to pass the time. Something non-
medical to discuss when we chat each week.

Poem For Kate In Absentia

We both know you're dying, though your husband
still has faith, and you cling to his hope, coming back
week after week because it makes his life bearable.

When the chemo bags are empty, and the stories read,
you leave the pages behind for a needful stranger.
In 2000, when you lost your breast,
your husband insisted you have chemo then, too.
"It makes me feel more dead than alive,"
you confessed to me after the first week.

Appointment days, you'd leave the house,
drive to the woods, walk the trails instead of
treatment, those huge redwood trees shading
your path.

Each evening you'd return to your
husband's innocent embrace.

You made me promise not to tell. And
I never did, until now.

Your husband has fallen in love.
He says she's a lot like you. A painter
he met in a bar. They danced all night.

Just like the two of you, at that dive bar
in Santa Fe (when you called at 3am to say
you'd finally met someone).

When he came to visit, your husband
stayed here. His new love lives close by.
He returned from her arms, all sparkly, school-
boy giddy. Not like last year,

when he was walking wounded, watching
his cell-phone video of your forest burial,
over and over (the one I still can't get
out of my head).

Your husband has fallen in love. But she's
married and her spouse is abusive, although
he's 'never touched her.' "She's ready
to leave him," your husband says.

I tell him about our friend, Lynnie,
whose husband 'never touched her,' either,
until she tried to leave and he shot her
twice in the head.

And there's your voice in my ear, Kate.
Watch out for my husband, you whisper.
He's always been naive.

For Kate O'Donnell, (1949-2014)

published in The Nashville Review, 2017

HAIBUN FOR KATE WHO IS DYING

You step out of the Benz, grab your carry-on, about to be swallowed by the throng pouring into Terminal 1. Your white-fringed head sports new growth after the latest round of radiation. You look like the Buddhist nun you've always carried inside of you. I hug you goodbye for the fifth time. You pull back and your eyes pin mine, bore into me like panic, like love. I read your thoughts. You memorize my face. I hold your gaze in my throat.

Amazon strong, one
breast gone, one foot in the grave,
her desperate smile.

Published in KYSO Flash 2017

82 Miles From the Beach, We Order The Lobster At Clear Lake Cafe

The neon flashes "Lobster" and "Fresh!"
The parking lot is crowded. We've been driving since dawn.

The lobster must be good here, you say.

The harried, Korean waitress seats us near the kitchen.
She's somewhere between forty and dead.

I show you the strand of her coarse, black hair
stuck between the pages of my menu.

Undeterred, you order the lobster for two.

I investigate the salad bar.

Yellow grease pools in the dregs of blue cheese dressing;
a small roach skims the edge.

Before the waitress can bring the clam chowder, I kick you under the table.

I'm sorry, I say brightly. *We've changed our minds.*
I'm responsible for the look of defeat on her face.

As I head out, you stop and leave a twenty on the table.

I have never loved you more.

Published in Slipstream, 2017

HONORABLE MENTIONS

Frank Kearns
Downey, CA

Morning Ghazal for Poison Ivy

A chameleon glowing green to rusty red, that's poison ivy
From early Spring to first snow-fall, many shades of threat, that poison ivy

A snake that seeks the sun along a damp road waiting
as walkers pass their boots across the edge, that's poison ivy

Heat lamp like a desert sun burned the blisters dry as I,
a restless child, lay confined in bed by poison ivy

My brother fell from the elm tree once—
of all the things he learned to dread, it wasn't poison ivy

At my mother's funeral, regrets appear
on the edge of words, unsaid, like poison ivy

Listen Francis Xavier, savor the light this morning
through dream-born half-flight, free of ghosts,
and that bastard poison ivy.

Again

after Joy Harjo

No matter what, we must cry to live
a family around a chrome-legged table
farmhouse groaning under winter wind
an empty chair, the sudden end of a world

No matter what, we must eat to live
the world a scared pine table
two of us in a cramped kitchen
that was one beginning
one long ago world

No matter what, we must shed our skin to live
at a maple table a few steps from the kitchen
morning light splashing
across the scratched wood floor
The world can begin here, at this table

where we two can say what can only be said here
as a day, a year, a world long enough to be a life
folds into the beginnings and endings
that stretch beyond our comprehension
perhaps the world ends here
again, and again.

Henry Crawford
Silver Springs, MD

The Fruits of Famine

On those nights we traced
the shapes of fruit until the dark
became our eyes.

On those nights we left our fields
unhearing the crack of broken roots,
the silence of dying ground.

On those nights, twilight filled the deserts
of our crossing with the vermillion breath
of watermelon.

Driving by a Farm at a Distance –

A Pennsylvania farm knows
you're just driving through.
It sees your rolled-up windows
and lets you go. I sometimes imagine
waking up to a table of butter and milk,
my imaginary wife adorned in gingham.
Outside, imagined animals are waiting
for me to imagine them, too.
There might be pigs, but more likely
chickens. I imagine myself putting on
my farmer's suit to scatter some feed.
I believe there are machines that I imagine
need fixing. The heat of the day glistens
on my soaked bandana. My imaginary son
is in the next field, all blond cowlick,
stooped over a row of young corn.

Maybe he's a Four-H Club hero
or a desk-bound nerd who wants none of this.
But there's always an imaginary dock,
sometimes going out to a useless pond,
sometimes buried in the woods
by a dragonfly creek.

I am afraid of autumn.
It's then, I imagine, the evening
will appear to me: my plain wife
listening to the radio, some imagined music
in the farmhouse air. This is the night
I will stay on the dock. No one calls.
I lower myself into the flotsam
of leaf dust and spent butterfly wings
to fall with the stars under the surface
of imaginary water.

District Lit, October 11, 2019

On those nights, the stars seeded the skies
above the camp. Jackfruit guards
stood still as celery stalks.

On those nights we dreamed like you
of strawberry days on porcelain plates.

On those nights I made an apple out of sand
and watched it blow away.

First Place, 2019 World Food Day Poetry Competition

Making an Auto Insurance Claim

[my side view mirror] [got whacked] [by an unknown] [driver] [so I called] [an 800 number] [to make] [a claim] [and I was put] [on hold] [listening to a song] [with a strange] [xylophone] [solo] [and they broke in] [every three minutes] [to thank me] [for my patience] [I don't play] [the xylophone] [but I was in] [a band] [called] [Curb Your Dog] [with a drummer] [called] [Nutty Chuck] [he knew] [three notes] [on the xylophone] [C] [C#] [and D] [he could play them] [fast] [or] [slow] [but we had to] [kick him out] [so Nutty Chuck] [and a guy named Horse] [moved] [to California] [with the xylophone] [and around] [this time] [the phone] [was asking] [if I would like] [to take] [a survey] [at the completion] [of the call] [after which] [the song] [with the xylophone] [came back]

[there's always] [a tendency] [to account] [for things] [my aunt Grace] [who was not] [my real aunt] [learned to play] [the flute] [at the age] [of 98] [I remember] [asking her] [about] [my mother] [as she talked] [she would toot] [a note] [or two] [she told] [my mother] [toot toot] [my dad] [would never] [toot toot] [leave his wife] [so all] [the children] [toot] [toot] [toot] [would be] [illegitimate] [toot] [toot] [my mother] [almost took] [her own life] [toot] [when she learned] [she was pregnant] [with me] [toot] [toot] [Grace said] [I should be] [grateful] [they didn't have] [abortion] [in those days] [I tooted back] [I'd be good] [either way] [toot] [to you] [and now] [the phone] [began] [asking questions] [I gave a 7] [to the service rep] [I gave 0] [for the time] [on hold] [I gave my mom] [an 8] [I gave myself a 9] [for being patient] [and 10 for the song] [with the] [xylophone] [solo]

Honorable Mention, Wergle Flomp Humor Poetry Contest 2019

INTERVIEW

THE POET KING OF
PASADENA-SAN GABRIEL VALLEY
DON CAMPBELL

Interview by Coco

Raindog

If you are part of the poetry scene then chances are you've heard of Don Kingfisher Campbell. Local Editor-in-Chief of Small Press Lit Mag Spectrum Publishing. This San Gabriel born and raised poet has an "MFA in Creative Writing from Antioch University Los Angeles, listed on Poets & Writers, founder of POETRY people youth writing workshops; publisher of Spectrum magazine; leader of the Emerging Urban Poets writing and Deep Critique workshops; and host of the Saturday Afternoon Poetry reading series in Pasadena, California. Mr. Campbell has taught Creative Writing in the Upward Bound program at Occidental College and been a Guest Teacher for the Los Angeles Unified School District for 35 years. Want a poet in your classroom, library, bookstore, coffeehouse, or event? Please email: *donkingfishercampbell@gmail.com* in accordance to his online bio.

In the past Don has been a Board Member and Los Angeles Area Coordinator for California Poets in the Schools program. Don was also a teaching poet for the Red Hen Press Writers in the Schools program as well. It is Don's philosophy to *"regularly bring writers as guests into my classes."* Another humbling position within the community has been to be the host of poetry readings and workshops in Pasadena for over twenty years and was commissioned $400.00 to record an original poem *"Three-sixty from an Artistic Seat"* for a City Speaks art exhibit in Pasadena. Campbell stated it was "The most money I ever made from a poem."

As a poet this was my first time reading my poetry to a group of students. It was as surreal experience to say the least! It halfway felt like a runway red carpet dream, and a Freddy Kruger Nightmare on Elm Street!

There they were a classroom of about 15-20 all hanging on my words like I was some kind of poetry star! I wasn't sure what to expect in preparing for this function, so I brought my normal Unicorn Coco necessities; my pink microphone that I take everywhere, my phone w/ stand, a red bull, all of my poetry, snacks and

Although this was my "star" moment I felt more like a crazy bag lady that just came in and crashed the classroom. "Wanna hear some poems little kiddies? I got a humdinger here for you!" an inner monologue I do my best to ignore. What made things even more nerve racking was the poem Don & I choose for this Spectrum Special Edition was "Would You Notice Me?" my soon to be famed poem on suicidal ideation. Oh joy! Trigger warning (no pun intended).

Lucky for me I wasn't the only poet asked to come read that day. Fellow Spectrum Publishing and frequently published INSCAPE poet Mark Fisher was also asked to participate. The subject matter of his poem "fallow" also a somber tone. We all wore blue that day as if some type of symbolic message of grief, mourning, and despair. Actually, it was simply mere coincidence that we all chose the color of the day to mirror the depths of sorrow within our written verses. The teens spoke softly taking small breaths to conserve air and prevent choking on the fumes of our words. "Do you ever get writer's block?" one asked me as I quickly replied, "Nope! To many voices in my head for that." Anyone who struggles with Depression or PTSD like I do understand the weight of that statement. The constant battles with myself, writing feverishly in efforts to appease and quite the sirens singing to me.

The experience is still one I only half believe I had. Like I imprinted my immortality in the words they carried, stamped in memory and parchment permanence.

When asked *"What would you like your business cards to say?"* the extremely charismatic and quick-witted Don Kingfisher Campbell jokingly replied; *"Poetry Genius...ha ha ha."* as the wheels of time spin backwards in his mind he recalls *"When I was younger they used to call me the Poetry Guru of the San Gabriel Valley,"* some 20 years ago.

By now curiosity had me question; *"What prompted you to become a poet?"* As if the Bad Co black t-shirt didn't already say it all, *"Rock Lyrics."* replied Campbell.

As the head banging begins Don recites: *"Yes, Pink Floyd, Led Zeppelin. Then in college I learned about real poets, or lyrics without external music, but rich in internal muse."* If you are good at math and paid attention to how old Campbell was in the picture above, you'd know that college was in the 80's for him, "1981-1984" to be precise. While in college at CSULA Don began to reminisce about his fondest moments of being part of "Cal State L.A.'s literary magazine, … Statement magazine in college." Don remembers being an Edi-

tor where he "made some rad changes there too! I love wrap around covers…I love putting the logo in a different place each time. Each issue had its own flavor." A format he would carry through into Spectrum Publishing. Proud of his life achievements Campbell reveals that he *"received MFA at 53."*

In discussing Don's illustrious career during the interview, he surprised me by revealing *"I just posted my reviews of over 60 books of poetry I read for my MFA on your page. Enjoy!"* Christmas came early for me as I replied with *"THIS IS AMAZING!!! EEEEEEEPPPPP!!! Best Christmas present EVER!!!"* I buoyantly clamored. Once I came back down to earth with a galaxy of stars in my eyes, beaming in yearning, practically salivating at the thought of getting my own golden ticket. I asked about his MFA from Antioch, *"is that like Deeeee place? Seems like a lot of MFA's come out of there."* Don assured me, "The LA place, for sure." Still aboard the inquisitive train I docked at the station inquiring; *" who would you say are your top 5 writers that influenced you?"* I was deeply and delightfully surprised that none of the traditional "Poe, Dickens, Whitman, or Shakespeare where on the list that follows as:

James Tate
Stephen Crane
Gregory Corso
Henri Coulette
Douglas Adams
and Michele Serros

"Ooops, that's six" proclaiming that he could name more and when asked who the favorite was stated *"Six-way tie."* Sounding a lot like me when I'm asked what's my favorite Michael Jackson song, or which of my two sons' is the "favorite." Upon looking up each of the poets listed I then pondered and asked, *"then what is the most important book you feel every poet should read, and why?"* Without pause or hesitation Don relishes in his answer, *"Poem-*

crazy by Susan Woolridge . She gets into the why and how of doing poetry."

This is exactly how I felt about Don. The way he crafts a poem is unique in the manner that he can turn any thought, experience, or object into a poem. The whimsical nature of his poetry tickles my spirit into admiration. Don has a way of teaching, leading and mentoring that is so unconventional that most don't even realize that each pen stroke onto paper is guided by his hand. Poets feel safe to express themselves freely, an openly, with no fears of judgment. Wraps each person in a warm blanket of acceptance and support. My curiosity left me so thirsty for the knowledge which he possessed. I had to know more! I had to know where the fountain of his talents was hidden and how it came to be.

What sparked Don's inspiration to take this journey of responsibility to the promise land of immortal verse. Don walks you across the tightrope of instruction as if the crocodiles that snap at our feet aren't there. Those insidious fears of not good enough, thoughts of insignificance, of untalented refuse dissipate in his navigation of one foot in front of the other. The audacious realization once upon the other side that you made it across! Not only did you make it across but you now posses the ability, the language, the talents to cross again on your own. Gathering the items in the forest of desire the means for survival in the literary world.

I became a published writer, an artist, a photographer, a reputable member of the literary community because Don was there each step of the way. Don has paved the way for so many well respected, award winning, laureate obtaining, poets and writers that when I went to last years Lit Fest just about every panel had a Spectrum published poet! Don never boasts or brags about any of his acquaintances or achievements, and Don's accolades are many! When I posed the request, "would you mind giving me a timeline of your work? First Chapbook, First Book, Anthology, Collection?" he responded with, "OMG." Being privy to a slice of his works in a previous workshop I couldn't help but ask and answer him back with "I know right?!?! I still have the picture from the workshop but not sure that's everything."

"Not nearly. I have produced over 50, maybe 100 chapbooks over the last 40 years. Usually 4 a year." Can you say LIFE GOALS!!! Don did his best to recall the first of first; "First Chapbook: First Thoughts, 1981, First Book: Enter, 2002, Anthology: Statement Magazine, 1984, Collection: Room And Memories, 1998:." If I had the money, I would purchase every single chap book, perfect bound book, and collection that he has ever written. My favorite of favorites to date would be his book titled "The Planet of the Oreo's." With over 87 miraculous pieces. One of which was featured online for INSCAPE's moon-moon collection titled "Moon Poetry" towards the bottom of the page. Although my most favorite piece is "13 Ways of Looking at Little Chocolate Doughnuts" Don brings some of his books to readings and Spectrum workshops, however those looking to purchase his work should visit the Spectrum website – https://spectrumpublishing.blogspot.com/ or to see the vast list of Don's award winning poetry visit http://dkc1031.blogspot.com/ . Don's most recent achievement was receiving a "Partnership Award" from Los Angeles Poet's Society founding member Jessica M. Wilson this past November where they celebrated their 10 year anniversary.

Don welcomes all the poets of the Spectrum to his publication as well as the weekly meetings at the Santa Catalina Branch library here in Pasadena every Saturday from 3pm to 5pm. When I asked Don "In your own words why is your Publication called Spectrum?" The answer exquisitely simple and just, "Inclusive of everyone." Encouraging all voices to be heard and celebrated. In the most recent

Spectrum Publishing anthologies there were well over 60 contributing authors and artist! The little small press publication is growing begging to ask;

"What's the hardest part of being Editor-In-Chief for Spectrum?"

"Revisions sent in by poets to their poems."

"aww I bet that's frustrating."

"Seems like they could have finished their poems before they sent them in."

A lesson in courtesy for future contributors to heed. Don is a very patient, kind, understanding and considerate human being. So that being said I encourage future and current writers to value the time and commitment it takes to put together an anthology by getting submissions in on time and free of any needed additional edits. Make sure it is polished and ready for submission before deciding to submit.

"Why then do you continue to do it? What keeps you going?"

"I am a poetryholic. I never tire of finding interesting poems."

Knowing that feeling of drunken stupor from drinking in words I giggle to myself. Finally, someone else who appreciates not just the words written on the page but the people and experiences behind them. In closing I extended an invitation to share openly:

"What else do you want the PCC students and the world to know about you?"

"Advice I give anyone: if you feel out of place, own it, and strut around without hesitation.

Make them accept you with your confidence. I think you know that already.

Read the poems. They will tell you all you need to know...about me.

Read each other's work.

Support each other."

My ending statement to him... *"You inspire me sir."*

Nancy Shiffrin's books

THE VAST UNKNOWING poems
https://www.barnesandnoble.com/w/
vast-unknowing-nancy-shiffrin/1024165568

OUT OF THE GARDEN/novel
INVOKING ANAIS NIN/essay
GAME WITH VARIATIONS/poems

FLIGHT/poems https://www.lulu.com/search?
adult_audience_rating=00&q=Nancy+Shiffrin

CREATIVE WRITING SERVICES
http://home.earthlink.net/~nshiffrin

nshiffrin!@earthlink.net

TK Major WebWorks

→ Site design and maintenance
→ Publications / CMS / blogs
→ Wordpress specialist
→ E-commerce
→ Data-driven sites
→ Social media integration

Present your art or product, promote yourself, sell merchandise, even sell e-books, spoken word, music, or other downloads directly from your website. Integrate your social media presence with your site. Build a community right in your own website.

www.TKMajor.com
1.562.735.4075

POETRY II

Argos MacCallum

Prayer for Birds

for Jean

where the night hawk where the quail
where the owl of my dreaming destiny
spread your wings my bright bird
one for patience one for joy

in an orchestra of stoic locusts
a red headed finch swivels as a weather-vane
a gang of crows escorts the moon
in grand arrival and will yet again

the marble moan of the dove
a groan of a work-stooped woman
a workman's whistle sings the thrush
open the gate open the clouds

the cry of the perching thrasher
throws down sequins on the forest floor
high stakes and a card deck of feathers
stripes of light and silhouettes of rain

an almanac of angels revolves in the sky

Raindog

Two by Mike Mahoney

How Many Of Us Ever Realize
Ever Understand The Broken Truth:

that
far
too
many
of
us
have
far
more
words
than
experience
for
all the things we supposedly
dream, love, believe
& pray for?
all the things we supposedly
work, war, submit to,
sacrifice
& suffer for?

Even If It Doesn't Matter

even if it doesn't matter
one bit
in the end,
that doesn't matter
either
because nothing will matter
one bit
in the end.
so do it,
whatever you do,
whatever your dreams scream
at you to do
& do it right:
do the goddamn shit out of it.

abandon all fears,
all excuses.
abandon all reasons
why not

Two by Adrian Manning

Four Minutes

walking through the underpass
past the drunks and the stink of their cheap piss
like a droog with a wide open grin
and a look of blank, frightened wilderness
I thought I saw you in the gaping light
at the mouth of the deafening tunnel
smiling and waving and
calling my name
but it was all just a vision of heaven or hell
and the cops moved us on
as they knew time was fading
and the cars screeched on past with no intention
of stopping
on fire and melting and belching out fumes
that smoked, choked and enveloped us
it was all happening too soon
and I miss you, you're beautiful
and the sky weeps with darkness
as the freaks, the geeks, the ones with no hair
crowd us and drown us and deprive us of air
four minutes until the siren
breaks down
four minutes until we lose all sound
four minutes until the mountains collapse
four minutes or less perhaps
a girl in a sundress came
laughing along the pavement
she threw her arms open and begged for forgiveness
but I had none to give
and I shouted at her
forgive me, forget me, what is it worth?
I saw you in a record store
holding up vinyl from yesterday
old songs rolled around my head and my mind simply
laughed at that

it was cold, I was tired and I felt like a whisper
my eyes were closed and my childhood grew nearer
I love you, I need you, that's all I've got
its over, I've lived it, that was the lot
four minutes that's all we've got
four minutes...
four ...

Oh Death

you thief,
sliding in amongst
the shadows of
night,
stealer of time,
why do you
come around again
so soon?

gnawing at the edges
of me
reminding me of
your presence
as if I could ever
forget

your teeth marks
and scars
are constant
still painful
no matter how they
have aged

I know you are there
I always know
and the closer
you come
the more I will
ready myself
for the fight

be ready
I don't plan on
making it easy
why should
I?

DS Maolalai

A stretch.

the drinking
drove us
like tied boats
on tide-lines. we were in a bar
near my place - this local dive; the dice.
they served staro, franz
and various whiskeys
set to bad indie music
and seats arranged
outside.

it was a good place
to be for a while.
and there was
conversation, and
what our parents called
a stretch,
and stretch is the right word
too - we sat out,
smoking and watching trams
and traffic,
as it stitched
the hours
to daylight.

the sun played out
dusty,
like a shirt
on a half broken
clotheshorse,
drying on a hot
afternoon.

Georgia Santa Maria

A Dry Place

In New Mexico, old wood dries out,
lightens, gets papery, give off dust,
lightens in its weight and color,
knocks hollow to the hammer,
spits the old nails out,

rust to dust. The spiders love adobe,
their webs stretched taught,
a hiding place behind the old
cracked plaster, quiet, dark and stolid.
Paint pales, cracks and peels off.

The occasional rain will swell
and loosen it from the wood—
the colors faded, like a
memory of their former self.

The old glass windows, liquid,
pour themselves in waves,
the sand dots of imperfection,
bubbles, the ancient air of another time.
The glazing dries, falls out, they are
left tenuous as a leaf in winter

without human help. Restorations,
interference, the crumbling dirt
sifting always through the cracks.
The baseboards bulge, filling up.

A layer of Walmart plastic mitigates the cold,
holds the wind out just a little—
The crumbling wall that kept
the thieves and Comanches out
threatens at last to fall.

The pear trees blacken
and succumb to drought.

Two by Richard Martin

Skylight

The moon inched across the skylight
like a luminescent bug.
I remember that, the feel of it,
lightly on my eyelids.
It had started to rain
without any clouds.
The moon played in the rain
with friends in the yard,
friends that squirmed in the dark,
exchanged phone numbers
and good books with each other.
The moon was partial to Kafka,
the frozen sea inside of me.

It was not a dream.
Prior to bed, the moon sat in my desk chair.
It was brighter than usual and quite talkative.
"Space is a function of the mind," it said. "Space
doesn't have a personal identity."

Night warned me about the moon.
"It's no Romeo. Kafka
is not the right author for you.
You're afraid of bugs."
Night desired love.
I was burning up
and tapped my wife on the shoulder.
My wife took my temperature,
danced with the moon.
They laughed and talked,
split a bottle of rum.

"I'm dreaming," my wife said to the moon.
"No, he's dreaming," the moon said.
"I'm not dreaming," I said.

The moon paced the bedroom floor,
tried on the clothes in my closet.
It looked good in a suit and tie,
a wig or fedora would have helped.
The moon laddered to the top of the sky.
It lingered there, watching me
as a dream now.

Hoax Bubble

Here's what these words mean.
You're riding a horse into a Montana sunset.
Bleached bones entangled with meandering stars.
A call for order in a coyote's eyes.
Brick mountains and insufferable equations.

You could whistle a tune by Mozart.
Join the cause.
Enough dead in Afghanistan.
Media speak and lost mothers harmonize.
Language is a tattletale.

Now for the sands of incomprehension.
At the Alphabet Hotel, a botched press conference.
Sacred routes plotted for double-crossed chemicals.
Europeans consider Americans stupid.
Babble in the neo-cortex.

Two by Mary McGinnis

Sequins
(Blues for J.)

Soon he will be dead. He was having
electric stim treatments but only the shadow
queen understands his speech. It is
untidy now guttural and,
irritatingly blurred. The red
night dress hangs on him now, a
sad bubble of sequins coming unglued. The

square hands of his last lover
trembled in that
mesh of emptiness surrounding his body.
Quietly he closed their piano,
undid the red sash.
I make a sound in his name, as the
night takes over, and the scarecrow
sleeps, his mouth full of pens.

Because Of Birds

When I was nebulous and tiny in my mother's womb,
a crow sat outside her kitchen window and laughed.

When I was born, and my father's face was pocked with worry,
my mother hollered at the crow who kept laughing

as they plummeted down the road to the hospital in the rain,
and my mother felt the crow's wings beating against her back

and told no one. Then I came out of my mother's
steep, little cave, burning from too much light

and blue with resistance. I was born early
with a split cry, and was lost in glass and metal

until a priest in a dark crow coat
came in with the nurse and told my mother
she could take me home.

In Pennsylvania, hearing mourning doves,
I learned to love my suburban street of trees.

Then it was the raven, streaking across the sky,
with trash streaming down from her tail,

that made my life better: I learned
space had anchors, places where you could rest

Raindog

before tumbling into blackness. If I was patient,
the laugh of the raven was a bright piece of foil

jolting me awake. I stood straight,
listening for that spacious, honking laugh.

Once when we made love,
what was between us fluttered, a bird without a voice.

Neither of us attempted to make it stay.
Laughter was behind me like a splint no longer needed.

David McIntire

What I Really Mean Is...

i'm just tired

tired of trying to smile
tired of finding broken on my tongue
of laughter disappearing in the slipstream
of pretending to know how

i'm just tired

tired of weakness like a flag in a hurricane
of the grinning stricture that folds in on itself
of the weight of the sky
of the weight of paper thin sympathy

G. Murray Thomas

i'm just tired

tired of being the smartest fool in the room
of waiting on all the promises of joy
lain vainly upon my doorstep
of my point being missed
of my pint being empty

i'm just tired

tired of treading water every damned day
of pretending to understand the melody
tired of feeling absent from my own life
tired of every handrail on every bridge
tired of all the sharpened possibilities and their siren call
tired of the deepest wells
and the highest cliffs
tired of the pill-fed plausibilities
tired of the darkness holding so much sway that my masts become almost horizontal
tired of the anthems i am compelled to hum endlessly
i'm tired of the knowing
of the emotional quicksand
of the dream shards underfoot
i'm tired of the needing
and the never understanding
and the blood in my teeth
the air heavy with humanity
of the pavement forever soft with our failures
i am tired of the emotional labor of simply walking through this world

i'm just tired

Three by Basia Miller

The Camassia Natural Area: Bridges and Birdhouses

On a basalt lava cliff,
on a trail silenced and softened
by recent rain,

I pass berry-bushes, vines and grasses
thriving in
the persisting drizzle.

I'm drawn to the timeless space.
I could cede myself
and become a part of it.

I could disappear among the drooping fronds
of dew-dappled ferns
and green moss-covered trees.

Suddenly appears a posted metal sign
Wildlife & Riparian Habitat
that shakes me from my trance.

So I'm not here alone. The shrubs and trees,
the satin-gray igneous rock, the violent
angles of descent—all have their guardians.

I Feel My Prayers

Most often I give divinity a sidelong glance,
I resist acknowledging the unknown.
I hope everything goes okay, I say
or close an email with a cliche, *May you be well.*
These pass for common currency but hide a prayer.
They're like old books with ancient flowers pressed
between the pages.

My body is better at prayer than my words are.
My nerves tense up when my granddaughter begins to
cross the mountain stream. My muscles mimic hers
as her bare foot reaches for a flat rock, far but not too far.
While she's in-between, off-kilter, a wish wells up in me
to offer her a rail, *May she be safe.*
I steady her with my eyes, then tears roll down one by one,
stinging my eyelashes and cheeks.
May these seeds of prayer
support her in the instant and still be there
when she catches her balance again.

Clear-eyed now, I see other signs
of gentle caring for the landscape: long planks
bridge a rivulet to join weedy slopes,

wrens, chickadees, juncos and tiny tits
fly from the underbrush like Ferris wheels
to finally reach the feeders.

To my gratitude for this amazing place.
I add my special admiration
of all who tend its bridges and birdhouses.

*The Camassia Natural Area
is in West Linn, Oregon.*

On Reading John Hastings' Diary from Wilson, Kansas, 1885

He carved the boy's name on the headstone
like you brand a calf's rump to say you have taken him home.

Sunlight flashes on the stalls, then the barn door closes.
Death, heavy as a bucket that an arm even with a winch

can't raise from the well, strained the couple's hearts
as they grieved the loss of little John, fifth child, only son.

To answer the weight Kate hoarded iron, the kitchen
a smithy abloom with fire where skillets became caskets

to enclose the pain. In a leather pocket diary John Senior risked
two or three words daily, in pencil so as not to tip the balance.
At my grandmother's birth a few years earlier he wrote,
"Baby born," followed by, "3 pence for nails." The world
was too uncertain to go poking around. John would read
his plumb-bob to know to shift a scaffold to left or right.

His sun-blackened skin flaked off on the roller towel.
What could he say? Crops failed. Wind flattened the alfafa.

Good times came too. Evenings, he and Kate often stood
together, proud to see the girls bringing in the cows.

From my book, The Next Village/Le prochain village

Anniversary of Her Funeral

I look at two robes hanging in my closet.
The brown-plaid flannel is mine, and
the blue cotton one belongs to my wife.
Wearing mine, I walk through the rooms,
and sometimes I miss her so much,
I imagine her steeping her bed time tea
as we camped in the Sequoias.

She loved those night, heavy with the decaying,
bark odor of the redwoods. In the morning,
she appeared in her blue robe, surveying
the wild rye stiff with a dusting of frost.
During spring, we camped in the desert,
firelight reflecting in her brown gaze, and
her robe carried the scent of smoldering pine.

Now, it smells of Tide, and the pockets full with
the memory of her hands, pushed deep, fisted
against the cold. Once I wrapped her bathrobe
around my pillow. I held it like I hugged her
in our tent as coyotes howled in the cottonwoods.
When I slip into her robe, I remember her arms
sliding from its sleeves to hold me.

It's no use to pack my sleeping bag, tent, or
Coleman stove. For we sleep out only in dreams
where memories drifts like campfire smoke.
After thirty years, she passed, and I think
it's one thing to find a woman who'll make love
with you. It's another when a woman in a blue robe
sits beside you every night for the rest of her life.

On the Drive to My Wife's Grave

I wore my wife's cloth wristband.
If she was wearing it, I'd call it a bracelet
because a man shouldn't wear a graceful cloth.

Funny, what comes to mind when wearing a wristlet
of the dead. Rubbing the cone-shaped shells, stitched
to the brown fabric, I recalled the love beads hippies put on.

In basic training, I boxed my bell bottom jeans and sent
them home. I kept a memory of the Grande Ballroom
and dancing solo in front of the band stand.

Parking, I remember the day my wife came
from the kitchen and sat next to me on the couch.
I held an empty cup and stared at the blank TV.

To her I was daydreaming; but I was back
in '71, packing for Nam. Beside me,
Smitty sang, "I'm the God of hellfire."

Later, he replaced me when I stood
among the soldiers with orders for Nam.
He died overseas, north of the Delta.

My wife knew nothing about that as she sat quietly
at my side until she could no longer stand my trance.
Shaking my arm, she called "Earth to Joe."

She kissed my ear. She hugged me until our hearts
felt each other. Then, she broke away and asked,
"Where did you go? You left me hugging air."

How did I explain those things? It was easier to say,
"I love your brown eyes," because as a non-combatant
I hadn't earned the right to drift back into wartime.

I didn't say much. We held hands, and I
looked at her through the haunting silhouette.

Two by Tony Moffeit

I Have Learned to Sleep and Dream Songs

in the dream i am having a beer
with kell robertson in a cafe
in a small town in new mexico
when a woman approaches our
booth and asks about the black
notebook beside me *what do
you have in there?* she asks
and i reply *my songs* and she
inquires further *would you
sing one of them?* and before
i can answer kell remarks
if you'll join me in my booth,

i'll sing one of them for you
so the woman slides into the
booth beside kell and kell
begins belting out a song that
i am obviously writing in
my dream, it's called "i get
along with you" kell is
singing it acapella no blood
red guitar and every word is
perfect every note is perfect
and the restaurant crowd is
amazed, clapping and singing
along with the chorus "i get
along with you" i am thinking
it can't get any better than this
but it does because the woman
who asked about the song and
joined kell in the booth
miraculously begins
inventing words to the song
begins singing a whole
new verse based on her life
and ending with "that's why
i get along with you" the
restaurant crowd is going nuts
clapping and singing along
with the chorus "that's why
i get along with you" and i'm
thinking it can't get any better
than this but it does because
another woman, two booths
down, takes the song on a
whole new spontaneous

adventure, after kell, after
the first woman, the second
woman belts out a version
based on her life, and ending
with "that's why i get along
with you" and now the song
is no longer my song, no
longer kell's song, no longer
the first woman's song, no
longer the second woman's
song, the song belongs to the
restaurant crowd, belongs to
the people who are yelling
and clapping and repeating
the chorus "that's why i get
along with you" the dream
ends with a shot of kell's face
detached but satisfied as if
to say, *i've been dead for
five years but i've still got it*

Equinox

a frontier mapped out
by heroes and villains
why the world is structured as it is
and how it works
people think this is the world but it isn't
the world is a bubble a fantasy
greater than reality
a cigarette thrown on the ground
by bogart in the maltese falcon
and those eyes that peer
through the fog
looking for the black bird

the poem as much a part of us
as the breath the sweat
the appetite
a movie of our life
with scenes and dialogue
a stream of consciousness
and unconsciousness
heart jumping through throat
the healer in his trance
attention to the breath

the evanescence
we're here for a little while
and then we're gone
another spring

the secret is in stretching
the moment
transcending time
using space as a vehicle

the image stolen
made immortal by
the lust for it
the image
set up
as a scat song
a riff
to see yourself framed
in negative
colors reversed
secrets revealed
as you listen to coltrane
with eyes closed
as if you can hear
the colors of his sound
equinox
and an hour
of light
stolen from the darkness
a solo of sleep
the day before yesterday
filtered through to
the day after tomorrow

Robert A. Morris

Innocence

Even back then, we locked the doors. We latched the deadbolts and propped
the windows shut, chained our bikes and closed the blinds. We lived in the
remnants of a burning house, heard our father's stories of Korea and Vietnam.

We were promised no new taxes and no more wars except for the big one that
everyone knew was coming. We shared classrooms and movies as a unified
humanity, undivided by laws or labels, brothers and sisters of common heartbeat

and soul. We shared water fountains and proms despite a past, shameful and
bloody, and left behind if only for a while. We had it good but knew it wouldn't

last. In summer, we roamed without boundaries, beyond the ball park and
through the cornfield, across the highway and underneath the bridge. We stared
at oil-slick nebulae, swirls the color of absinthe and iodine. We smashed bottles

against the concrete, dug up spear heads, and dismantled atoms. We gathered
fragments of glass with uncertain hands. We found marbles and peacock feathers,
a hazy Polaroid and a splinter of bone. We divided these like strange currency

and returned to the sunlight, eyes blinking in awe of a world, vast only in
comparison to our experience. We stood with an arrogance known only by the
young, unaware of the distance that we were carried and how far we had to fall.

Evan Myquest

The Un-woke

Please, let me sleep
Not enough hours in the day
You woke me up for this?
This is news?
What do you want me to say before coffee
The world is a crummy, lousy, no good place
Injustice everywhere
Sham society without morals
Workplace subjugation and indenture
Ethnic bigotry, racial profiling
Creeping totalitarianism
The list does go on
And now there is the most microscopic reaper of all
But you see, there's such a thing as
The proper amount of sleep
So wake me when the news is good
I won't be that hard to find
I won't be in bed, no, I will be under it
Begging the dog not to give me away

Raindog

Two by Linda Neal

Arabesque

Curls of moonlight unwind over the trees.
I expect nothing exceptional of the night,

don't think of myself as jaded,
but I've seen too many shiny apples,

a thousand radishes made into roses,
lonely on a tray of ice, too many little girls

standing in arabesque, hoping
by balancing, to capture a mother's heart.

There is always music playing behind walls,
a jazz riff or a soprano's silk

to drag me back to childhood and the dance,
to a room with a view of a rose garden

and a grandmother who taught me
to sing hymns and kneel down, all the way to God.

There were diaphanous curtains between the seasons.
It didn't seem strange to expect Spring to be kind.

The Wrinkled Face of the Rabbi

I've always been cautious of the wrinkled faces of priests and shamans,
I've never gone to the beach with any of them who sit in the hot sun baking,
reminiscing, swinging their legs from a wooden bench. I've seen them
walking like bulldogs along the wharves of ancient cities where I've traveled,
their mustaches curling down like the lessons their forebears delivered
to my ancestors.

In small European countries where the parts of me were conceived
these wise men uprooted beliefs and secreted their own souls
between pages in the worn leather books they used for ceremonial
myths between women and men who never wanted to marry and live
the lives their parents lived.

Their teachings were wrinkled and old, like their faces, and sometimes
I even believed they loved me, directly, just because tradition is full of continental drift
and words flowing like the tides onto many tongues, as if words and ships
were the same when they crossed borders and heavy seas in the midst of wars.

The rabbi who walks down my street is short
and needs to get a new dog. His bulldog is getting too fat to walk,
and the rabbi is getting too thin to continue to pull on the leash.

I watch them from the window by my desk, and some days
I want to walk out there and grab the leash and say,
See, this is how you walk a dog! But then I realize
I'm not so young any more myself.

Joseph Nicks

The Quiet Now

if I could just stop dying
for a moment
and breathe the wind
that sweeps across the fields,

look deep into
the canopy and see
the forest for the trees
and the trees for the forest,
green so richly thrust against the blue
and white of clouds,

the unapologetic purples, yellows, oranges
that paint the pallid desert
when the winter rains subside

flesh and blood lay low
here while they can,
starvation played
against predation
as their urgent life-clocks
tick away the seasons

is life only such a longed for thing
because it ends so soon?

Steven Meloan

normal

The Days of Reckoning are Speaking

Oh Big Daddy, who plucks peacock feathers in the Midday sun
Send forth your androidal missileer
Stop off at the Walla Walla for your plastic bottle of shocked water
Touch the fluorocarbon heavens with skyscraper fingers
Sing AVE MARIA on the banks of the Seine & the Passaic rivers
The days of reckoning Are Speaking.

From the World Bank to the West Bank, from a Serb to a Croat
A Tutu to a Hutu, a Shiite to a Sunni
Hitler to al-Assad & back again to Mussolini
The eyes of old men seasoned in stews of raw meat
Back & forth   an eye for an eye   to the fall of man
Moses throwing his tablets back to the sky.

In the common atom, rigor mortis speaks with futuristic eyes
Synchronizing brainwaves in silicon Valley
Drinking primordial soup on the moon
Viral bed bugs descending on the House of Congress
Pissoirs filled with the blood of poets
Sounds of the ManBeast licking his cryptogenic wounds
Sounds of the rivers   creeks   puddles seas.

Yesterday I watched a white dove fall from the sky
This morning it is raining bones & void promises
Smoke in the window, ash on the violets
Weeping ghosts upon the long Trail of tears
History rich with battered suitcases & one-way tickets
Merciless waves beat their fists upon the shore.

Days of reckoning
Days the clouds have open mouths
Days the clouds begin to speaks.

April/2020

Tom Obrzut

WE GOT EXACTLY WHAT WE WANTED

We got exactly what we wanted
And paid the right price
After the taco eating contest turned deadly
We were surfing the internet
Working on our emergence
As Myers-Briggs predicted
Jerry Seinfeld and Ellen Degeneres
Would rescue us in the airport

I just want things to work
It's all about tech and a 2 year guarantee
The internet is even better at our best deal
Injury law attorneys on the eye witness news

Protect our children
They are believing painful childhood secrets
We are knowing we're free
When the bell rings on a decent afternoon
That's how it's proven
The sound, the clarity
The destruction of a hurricane called life
That was predicted weather

We got exactly what we wanted
It wasn't cheap
The blessed virgin was crying
Tears of blood
But it wasn't broadcast until later
When the war was starting
The car was stalling
Everything became nothing

Then nothing again.

Two by Dean Okamura

Never the same sequence

Going on a hike
on the ocean trails
or the winding paths
of the preserve is
like reading a book
of poetry. I step
through nature and
some things settle
in my eye: the small
wildflowers after a
Spring rain, the tree limbs
swinging in the breeze, those
pelicans soaring in formation
patrolling the sea cliffs
in unison, a spout of
breath from a dolphin or
a whale, the patterns
they make on the ocean
surface, living life
in open waters. I stop
to gaze at poems in
a book, each a different
display of life, a chance
to experience a wonder
of existence. Never the
same sequence although
it is the same trail or book.
Do I pick them or
Do they pick me?

Dean Okamura

Dean
Okamura

Unannounced

Some seek
sacred destinations,
ceremonies,
people.

A quest for
blessing,
experience,
ecstasy.

All worthy things,
all heartfelt plans,
all outside the common
course of our lives.

Often, I arrive at the sacred
and find myself only
a curious observer.

Devotion,
gratitude,
desperation:
I see them.

Even my unprepared soul
can be moved.

Yet, the sacred seeks
and finds me elsewhere.

Unannounced,
thanks me,
comforts me,
lays strength on me.

At a time of stillness,
turmoil boiled over,
nothing more I can do.

Few words,
many tears,
far-reaching relief.

No advice,
no insight,
no message.

Mere presence.

Norman Olson

Cartoon Vampires in the Hallway of the Old Endicott Building

Vampires hang upside
down
in dark corners of the hallway,
cartoons with
bad breath. The hallway
stretches in yellow perspective
from the deli to abandoned
store fronts
with mirror windows.

NORMAN J. OLSON···Artist with special painting and drawing style

Norman Olson

We know that ghouls masturbate
each other behind the windows

and birth defects and insanity
kiss and fuck.

Old civil servants sit at
cracked Formica tables
and eat
taco salad. Their faces are
reflected in mirror windows
and in
undead
cartoon eyes.

Chasing Tail

Pop your collar
I have met the Mad Hatter

Have you?

Cut my lips on broken theories
lost my tongue
learned to shut up
and listen

Ears waxed with tomorrow's ashes
vital organs exposed in serenade

Laughing at the blood and licking
our way back to center plasma

Seven layers of smoke coat your lungs
I have witnessed all ten eruptions

Have you?

Enough poison fills those vials
to drown our final prayer in slumber

Morphine gods and silicone dreamers
plastic kisses and crystal groans

Scratches of sand sharpen focus
forced to shut up
and listen
dehydrated in the desert

The taste of halogen and furies
mute, burnt, spent, extinguished

Beneath the flames decrees fall silent
judgment has no value in a void

Stealth white rabbit safe with secrets
never will reveal what isn't sought

Burrowed in the cold forgotten earth
chewing on the cud of all our questions

Slate

Wipe me clean
without Clorox or bleach
just simple honesty

Sanitation is next to salvation
in some circles

Sacred vowels
squeak
ooh and ah
before sighing

Little spaces in the corner
dusted off
brought to surface
made to shine

Lord, help me find
the right words
to tithe

All I have
left to offer
are my dreams

Lorine Parks

Birds of America Plate CCXXXIX

i.

The dead bird lies on the blacktop
framed by cement bumpers
matted on tarmac
in a no-man's land between parking spaces

How it got here
what killed it or why it died
not apparent
Healthy-looking for a dead bird

Body plump like a duck
but green-lobed toes not webs there
so not a water fowl
Green legs   not like any duck

The black bird that lies in the parking lot
fixed and listless
is Plate CCXXXIX
Audubon's *fulica americana   The American Coot*

ii

Audubon's specimen has been dead only an hour
He's shot it and poses it on an upright board
his own invention   a grid bristling with wires
Flintlock set aside he tilts the model
he's god-like with his gift *yes   a little more*
picks up his brush

Inside the aquatinted field
the coot halts   one talon lifted in mid-step
It shifts its weight from green left leg to right
Slowly it advances to the sedge-lined pond
striped shins splayed out   breast low rump up
white tail exposed   Now it stretches out its neck
searching for succulent water-pea pods
chirping its short call *here   food here   come here*

Once he is sure his life-size drawing is complete
Audubon and his party eat it for their dinner
slow spit-roasted like yesterday's flamingo
but tender   more like canvasback or crane
And in the background

chattering in plaintive tenor tones
we saw what happened here   baa-uck bauk
baauck bauk
the shocked flock tiptoes off the folio page

Two by Simon Perchik

*

You can't tell from these clouds
why this afternoon was set on fire
is burning through some lullaby

you're singing to yourself
by gathering a few leaves, some twigs
for the gentleness falling out your mouth

—you dead know how it is, each hush
must be buried on the way back
with lips that bleed when rinsed in rainwater

leaving a sky that no longer takes root
is drifting into its hiding place
and each night listens for the word after word

returning as the small stones around you
that warm your hands, that listen the way smoke
reaches out from ashes and step by step.

*

You draw a star on the calendar
and without touching your lips
an unexpected breeze reminds you

there's now in writing where light
will slow down and the days take forever
to remember someone is holding your hand

embracing August the way a rock still alive
is broken in half and without a sound
added to the fire —it's a see-through star

and under your fingers forgets
it has a shadow just now starting out
will cover the Earth with a night

that goes on burning —you use a pencil
for its wood that knows nothing but corners
kept sharp even when turning to stone.

Jeannine M. Pitas

Postcard from Aliki

Thanos, Greece

Distant Mt. Athos won't let the soft-blue sky erase it.
It juts out, rocks and crags reminding me
that none of us will be here for too long.
Stained black rocks of charred Aliki,
parched brown and green. They can't
forget the wildfire that ravaged here
two years ago, burned the goat
path's railing away. Nor can the
turquoise-jeweled sea conceal
the bare rocks with sharp,
black beds of sea-urchin nails
waiting to trap human feet.
Ghost trees stand like dinosaur bones
in a museum, but at least they don't get
gawked at; they're passed over for those
that still pretend to be lush.
I send you a charred landscape, dust-brown
grass punctuated by a stone wall.
I give you the incessant call of sheep's bells,
the chatter of cicadas that won't let you sleep,
the din of bees and flies along the parched riverbed.
I send you the smell of octopus tentacles, of
fish bones carcassing the beach.
I offer you whatever gods still skulk
among the gray-white temple ruins
and abandoned marble quarries, scowling
at the shirtless tourists who snap
incessant photos, who bear no oblations.
It's only a matter of time before
dry lightning returns, before the whole mass
of dirt and rocks and roots
bursts again into flame.

D. A. Pratt

Nothing's normal

In the early twenty-first century
things look normal –
but they're not …
There is nothing normal
about today's politics
around the world – especially
in North America …
There's nothing normal

Jen Dunford

about today's obscene
allocation of resources
both financial and whatever else
we call "resources" …
Nothing's normal
about how little we value
the planet's environment …
Nothing's normal
about how much deference
we give to outrageous positions –
especially in the areas
of the religious and political …
Nothing's normal
about our tolerance
of idiotic views in general –
they're idiotic and ought to be
"called out" for being idiotic …
Nothing's normal
about the treatment of girls and women
in the twenty-first century (still an issue!) …
Nothing's normal
about ethnic and racial relations
in the twenty-first century (say it ain't so!) …
Nothing's normal about … hell
what's to be written?
Nothing's normal … and if
you think things are normal
you are part of the problem.

Lauren S. Reynolds

Rebecca, Ascending

No judgment
from the sky
when Rebecca jumped.

Still, was the air.
Swiftly did the robin
swoop and flap,
as he had when she climbed
up the silo's slender
neck.

Still, the trees said nothing.
Still, clouds took no notice.
Here, she understood
the power of being
insignificant.
of going on being,
and not being…
of keeping plans.
of having resolve.

She jumped up,
as she had intended,
out at the sun.
But being
not a bird,
Rebecca knew,
that gravity comes
to all things
ascending.

Two by Kevin Ridgeway

BAD DREAMS COME TRUE

she insisted I was a mystery to her:
my brooding intensity
and the assault of thoughts, feelings
and my distorted creative visions
overwhelmed her for nine years.
I cannot remember our last kiss
after dinner at the bus stop
across the street, where
she helped me climb onto the bus.
I was passed out cold when she tried
to call me at midnight once she realized
that she was dying and wanted
to tell me she loved me
when she told me goodbye
and now I am left standing here
until I can solve the mystery
of the man she left behind.

QUARANTINE #9

I am in a screaming match
with the motherfucker next door
both of us mad dogging each other
from windows in locked down houses
across from each other, bored
and paranoid and half naked.
we promise each other
if the world doesn't
come to an end,
we are going to fuck
each other up because
my Amazon Prime order
was delivered to him
by mistake, and to be
extra careful, he will not
give it to me because
of the possibility of
spreading infection,
and I can swear
I hear him watching
the movies I ordered
for myself as a way
to escape from
assholes like him.

Two by Brian Rihlmann

THINGS I'LL REMEMBER

the empty skies, streets, and shelves
signs on every shop door
how it snowed late on the flowers
already blooming
how the weight of it
broke certain branches
but not others
the jungle gym at the park
wrapped in yellow caution tape
vibrating slowly in the breeze
how that little boy cried
because he couldn't use the slide
how I sat on an empty bus bench
and watched the cars go by
studying the taut faces inside
some of them masked—
maybe all of them
how I reached out for my guitar
more often, remembering
how it cured me of more than one
panic attack, the steel strings
like a security blanket
how walking through my neighborhood
I felt the urge to wave
at every stranger passed
on the opposite sidewalk
how I reached out to people
I hadn't talked to in years
just to ask: how you doing?
how often I thought of those
whose fingertips I brush daily
at ATMs, doorknobs, gas pumps,
how we trade skin, DNA, our lives,
while picking fruit at the market
how we are the very air and sky
breathing each other every moment
whereas before, I trudged most days
completely alone, touching no one,
now I never felt so strangely…
connected

GHOST PASSENGER

Today, it's your ghost riding shotgun as I
head out to a long delayed appointment
with my old desert therapist, and as we
drive along, tires a song on the interstate,
I become your guide to her seeming emptiness,
her insights and her mysteries—
for she says nothing directly,
her whole landscape a parable...
the strange, broken shapes of her hills,
her crumbling pastel canyons,
how her clouds gather to drop sheets of rain
on sun baked playas. We follow the Truckee east,
and I explain how it flows from Tahoe,
and tumbles down the mountains,
across the desert, and empties into Pyramid Lake...
a landlocked river, never reaching the sea.
A living thread connecting two bodies
across this sagebrush basin
where an inland sea once stood.
Look, I say....you can see the lines on the hills,
watermarks where waves once lapped the shore,
and there...do you see him?
Halfway up, a wild mustang, standing alone.
Yes, I see him, you say.
He looks pretty shaggy, I say.
You look at him again, then at me.
You run your fingers playfully
through my graying chin whiskers,
and say he's beautiful, though...
and we both smile.

Cindy Rinne

Field of Vision

I.
Under volcanic
Blood Moon

two eyes fly and loop
like ribbons

past lava
in uncharted

canyons of fire opal
and silversword

Impermanent
octagons

of moss cling
to valley floor

Pupils enlarge
in elk silence

II.
Mountain goats

scale, then jump
land on a tiny ledge
with cloven hoofs

Sight limited
guilt forgotten
to only what is right
before them

III.
Visionary with bushy
brows and rabbit

eyes appears
behind clouds

Two by Christopher Robin

POEM FOR DOLLAR TREE, MOTEL 6 & LOSS

Dollar Tree I am craving the smell of my childhood Play Doh
Dollar Tree I think my cat may be missing
Dollar Tree I am sniffing your scented erasers
grape is my favorite....
Dollar Tree full of snot
heartbreak and apathy.....
Dollar Tree you show me no mercy
your toilet paper is too rough
and your restrooms always disgusting
or closed
Dollar Tree stuck behind Applebee's
and the Cineplex
and all the movie's are re-remakes
of remakes
of once terrible movies.....

Alexis Fancher

Dollar Tree I nearly sob in aisle 3
where the cat treats are

Dollar Tree you have never produced a decent snack
or a decent employee

Dollar Tree you are the religion of impermanence
and hollow plastic dreams

I see my reflection in a storefront window
and know I am deranged

spite, sweat and TV-commercial dreams
comfort me at the Motel 6

I give $20 to a homeless family
looking for a room-
he says he is looking for work
when I go to shake his hand he says,
"don't squeeze"
I make them promise if they come up with another fifty
and do get a room,
to please look for my cat
and describe her as, "fat, white, with a pink collar...."
they promise eagerly-
then disappear
and I slip further
into haphazard grief....

I am trying to sell the saxophones
of a dead best friend
I am trying to extend check out time

(everyone loves you when yer dead, Joe
but very few would love you to yer face....)

for three days I have been flat on my back
with moths flying out of my ears....

Joe, your face your shape your sneer
against the plain white wall
haphazard photos stuck to a purple poster board
with Dollar Tree glue

a dish of cat food sits in front of the poster board
untouched

Cleave

My girlfriend and her best friend, the bookstore owner
got into a drunken argument
over the word "cleave"

she arrived at my apartment at one a.m.

"she owes me fifty dollars" she said
"help me get my bags out of the car"

her friend doesn't let her
lie in bed and eat
peanut butter straight out of the jar

(but I secretly knew it was romance
she craved)

"I'm tired of being on," she said
"I need a break"

then she told me the bedroom smelled like urine

later I yelled at her that she'd been brainwashed
because her friend blasts NPR every morning
while she grinds the coffee

"So what, you're gonna vote for a democrat now?
What's gotten in to you?"

not a solid argument, considering she never
votes because she hates the government
even though she used to be rich
but I felt justified…

by noon the next day an old trick
had found her online
and offered her $900 for a weekend

She looked over at me

"Don't you work anymore?"

I didn't answer

"I don't like these pickles! They're too sweet!
What else ya got? Any candy?"

By the next week, all my charm had worn off

"I missed you," she said
"but now that I've seen you
I don't miss you anymore"

"Will you be back?" I asked

"I'm not sure," she said
and off in the Cadillac she went

John D. Robinson

SHIT TO DEAL WITH

The world is imploding
with Covid-19 ,
violence, disease,
suicides and wars,
the rent is due and the
food cupboard empty,
but there are poems
to write:
your partner is
leaving you and

Three by Judith Robinson

Buy A Ticket

An old, diminished town.
Broken streets, broken glass.
Walls here are layered
Many coats of paint, all peeling.
Flakes of rust glom on to any metal.
The salt does this.

A lone surprise amidst the grit:
A chrome-bright gym open
Twenty-four-seven for the afflicted
The jobless-wounded-welfare-ians who
Nagging at scabs, cannot sleep.

Someone says dance, someone says hope,
Someone says Wal Mart is coming;
Someone says try this, it will take off the edge
No one on the other side knows squat but

Of one truth the pounded-bruised-lacerated
Are certain---money would make everyone happy.

friends don't call
anymore, your dealer
is getting heavy and
you need to make
a hit,
somewhere,
poems are waiting to
be written,

but sometimes even
poets need to tell
poetry to back-off
so shit can be
dealt with.

this april

when the newborn doves
froze to death in their straw nest
on the window ledge
I was the mother who bore witness.
It was my window.

Renounce the Clairvoyant Child

pledge faith to sea,
its great depths,
its blueness, essential as the sky;
out West: there are Indians
in India: there are Indians;
trust in the clock, the calendar,
the time of warmth that follows chill;
this is what an hour consists of,
a day, a week, a month;
you have learned exactly why
you are here,
recognize what is tree
not brook, not bale, not Barry:
what you must climb so
as not to be mauled

then eaten

by what is called wolf.

Jean-Marie Romana

Sunken City

Kelp trees stretch to the surface in brackish water, taller than brick buildings,
    bulbs glistening;
dead man's fingers sprout from cracks in asphalt, swaying;
eels and octopodes in open windows lurk behind floating curtains;
unnamed fish dart through flotsam, stirred to a frenzy
every time an earthquake shakes the city like a snowglobe,
swirling plastic trash down to the depths of its lost metropolis.

Levi Romero

The Continuing Conversations of Pa and Falcon Eddie

a man at the duck pond
approaches me for a quarter.
for a bottle, he says.
a bottle of what? I ask.
a bottle of something to drink.
what's good these days? I tell him.
Importers, he replies.
that's what killed my friend, I say.
sorry, man. he mumbles, then turns
and walks away.

three, four. no, five. wait. six ducks skitter by.

in times like these I want to call you up.
maybe you've already brought in a few cords of wood.
they say it's gonna be an early winter.
harshest winter we've had since the 50s.

Raindog

did you raise any turkeys this year? I ask you.
Thanksgiving is only a few weeks away.

it's as if I can hear your laughter over the phone,
teasing me about something you say I should've done.
or filling me in on the latest death
of someone we went to school with.
and, of course, asking why I haven't dropped in to visit.

what do you mean you don't have time to visit?
everyone's got time! you scold me.
well… I respond, cautiously
avoiding the snares you're laying out.

no, que well-ni-well!
you interrupt my excuse.

you gotta make time to visit.
you whisper, your voice gone low.
never know when one of us
ain't gonna be around.

ten. twelve. no, sixteen.
seventeen, twenty,
twenty-one, twenty-two ducks.

how are things going? you ask
pues, tu sabes. I respond
hay veces que el pato nada
y hay veces que ni agua bebe.

Two by Dave Roskos

FIVE FINGERED MARY
for Kid Kelly

When I was eight-teen I had a job as an auto mechanic's helper
at the Public Works Garage through Ronald Reagan's
Summer Jobs for Youth Program.
Every morning I had to spread this cat litter like
detergent on top of all the oil spills
& maggots from the garbage trucks.
Then I'd help the mechanics do lube jobs & oil changes.

My grandfather had worked there years earlier
as a garbage man & everyone remembered him.
He wasn't an easy man to forget,
had been a prize fighter in his youth,
& was punch drunk.

He was the neighborhood crazy old man,
would stand in the middle of the street & scream:
BURN DOWN THE SCHOOLS!
& always encouraged me to play hooky,
saying, *Skip a day, it's OK.*

Well the public works guys talked right out loud
in front of me about the time he left work early in a rage
because he found out my grandmother was having an affair,
but I knew all about it anyway because he'd bring
it up every time they argued,
stomping around the house
yelling *ADULTERY! ADULTERY!*
& she'd say *YEAH! HERE! HERE! YOU BASTARD!,*
giving him the five, & sometimes, the ten, fingered mary,
an insult of a gesture wherein you put your thumb to your nose
& wiggle your fingers back & forth.
If you're real angry you add your other hand
to double the impact.

Yeah, fuck you Marie!
he'd yell & walk out
the back door & sit on the porch,
the screen door
slamming
behind
him.

Hi Pop, I'd say
sitting next to him
& taking in the breeze.
*Hi Davey, goin' to school
today?* he'd ask,
& sensing my
indecision
would advise,
Skip a day, it's OK!

& I would,
sitting in the backyard
drinking my dad's budweisers
till he came home
& joined me--

sad, sad, sad,
that they're gone--
dead
in the
ground.

I Found Poetry

I found poetry
in the package
goods store,

then I found
poetry in the
seemingly simple
language spit
out by whores,

again, in the
conversation of
day laborers
& furniture
movers,

in the daily
log books
kept by
truck
drivers,

in the dirt
swept into the
corners of
loading
docks.

Two by Jen Dunford Roskos

my ex husband would scream at
cars that didn't slow at crosswalks
"run me over! I'll get into a good school…"

after we divorced he got hit by a car

got a big settlement

spent all the money
on crack

(accepted for publication in Gasconde Review #6)

at central beach

seagulls peck at garbage
greed flies bite my flesh
the only pen i brought
is running outta ink
and dede has been dead
one week one day and
that fat seagull is dancing
the hokey pokey and
dede's body has been
dead four days

is death the ultimate kick?

brain death a cessation of all
impulses and reflexes from
the reptile brain, the
primate brain, the
homosapien mind as if
her head was a jenga tower

and when fentanyl yanked out the base
she was not dede, legally deceased,
a breathing corpse kept alive
by machines - less alive than
a greenhead fly, a moon jellyfish,
a barnacle atop a
black-stained scallop

i feel as empty as this pen,
good for a few more letters,
each fly bite a tiny sword
stabbing flesh that still has feeling

she was vitality despite all the years
of addiction and sobriety piled up like a
shaky jenga tower and i stop

because my pen
like my friend
is dead

C.C. Russell

FRUIT OR VEGETABLE

1.

Mineral, vegetable,…

Everything.
  Stain on the new shirt.
  Ta Chien chicken.
   Celery sauce.

Everything.
  The spice that it takes to burn this
   off of the tongue.

2.

Maybe villanelle for
two carrots
and a pear.

Sestina
for three apples
and bitter kale?

3.

There were strawberries
that summer.

For breakfast, we would fill a bowl
with them, shower them
in sugar, drown them
in milk.

My father would eat his
over ice cream,

always the colder one.

4.

My garden was rhubarb
and cabbage,

bitter
and sour.

5.

So this apricot and artichoke
walk into a bar…

6.

The joke is in the telling;
a drone on the other side
of sunset.

Your voice
on the phone that night,

thick

with ferment.

Previously published in Whiskey Island, 2017

Patricia Scruggs

Reframed

She's mounting the photo in a new frame.
"My dad," she says. "I found it tacked to his wall
next to a citation for bravery at Guadalcanal.

Gallantly assisted in the rescue of the wounded
under heavy fire from the enemy.

"That's who I want to remember. This young sergeant.
Not the man we learned to hide from when he got drunk."
She lays down her pliers, stares out the window.
"It's a wonder any of us are sane."

As she fits the frame over the picture, the glass snaps.
"Shoot," she says. "That's the second time.
Further proof. My father
destroys everything he touches."

Arianna Sebo

The Book of Moths

The moths have their own religion   but we try
one of colour and flight   with Sunday school children
fuzzy feelers searching for luminescence and church bazaars
not so different from us humans   Sunday sermons and tapioca pudding
following our flights of fancy   searching for heights
allowing our imaginations   and falling from grace
to pave the way for our good intentions   like the moths
not always fulfilled   obsessed with the light

(*first published at The Coachella Review April 10, 2020*)

Lisa Segal

ASSEMBLY REQUIRED

The small pile of metal
on the work bench in front of me—
funnel-headed Titus screws
and M6 mounting hardware—
allows me to make
cam lock and nut connections.
Regardless of the sales pitch,
everything comes with some assembly required

Unbalanced necessities rock me.
Whether I like it or not,
I'm post-Beckett.
Appropriateness is now but a whisper.
Previous formalities speak nothing
to my contemporary tremors.

It's so hard to hear.
Please.
Scratch through.
Touch me.

Renee M. Sgroi

On memory

(after Kwame Dawes' "Sorrow")

It is like the fine dust, we find:
over everything, a dust that infiltrates
nose and lungs and like a cloud of smoke
stifles. It is the morning
sorrow, swirled into coffee cups
and spread as grainy butter across
a burnt toast, breakfast ordinary in
the way a woman combs her hair
and sees white-grey lurking
at the temples, or a man's self-inflicting pat
of middle age given to the growing paunch.
This dust is purple
and blue and mixed with orange,
mélange of colour entices, frightens. It stokes
its own fires with ash and beckons nights
of five-fingered whiskeys. It is our dust
our sheddings, worn as multi-coloured blanket
or cloak we carry and spread out as Yeats
under others' feet, treading softly always
on the memory of our dreams.

*"On memory" first appeared in
Synaeresis 10, vol. 4 no. 3, April 2020*

Sanjeev Sethi

Audit

Repeated need
to scout for encomiums
on social media, and the like:
I wonder what unhealth snows us?

Inspissated emotions
fill diaries
or transmit
drill of disputes.

As with soldiers:
shrouded brave hearts
carry their political master's shame.
Pen warriors lug whose hot water?

Eric Paul Shaffer

How I Lost My Library Card

This kid at the library was reading aloud to himself in the corner,
and some old man reading the sports page--wasting time on men
who play with balls for money!--told the kid to shut up, a library,
he said, was supposed to be *quiet*, so *be* quiet, for God's sake,
and of course, in his mind, there was no doubt about who God was.

When I saw the poor kid's surprise, his embarrassment, his shame,
I finally spoke. I said, "Man, *you* shut up. Look, you grumpy fool,
what we have here is a kid reading. He's *reading*! These days,
that's a goddamn miracle. Thirteen hungry, homeless people live
on the library lawn, and you're upset because he's reading *aloud*?

Listen, you dumb bastard, silent reading is for the dead! Are you
hearing me? His lips are moving because those words are alive.
He's speaking aloud because what those words need to revive them
is his breath. He's using his voice because all that story needs
to be heard *is* his voice. So I have an idea. Toss the newspaper

in the trash, and go *play* some damn basketball, instead of sitting
on your flabby ass gazing at numbers about games you never saw.
And while you're at it, find this poor kid a chair, get him a platform,
a podium, a pulpit, put him on a pedestal to shout from his book
in the strongest voice he can raise, and ask him, no, *beg* him, to read

to you, to me, to the library staff, to the patrons, to the thirteen
ravaged souls on the street, and to the rest of this vast, distracted
nation. Let him read his book to us all and make us all one people
for once concerned about what really matters. Let his voice lead us
through a story we need to hear! Let him read! Just let him *read*!"

Alima Sherman

it's like a scent

sometimes this happens, when I open a door
that has been bolted for a long time.
a smell is trapped like bones that break
but leave with the body as it exits, not looking back
yet, something remains, even more alive
allows the sensations particular to that space
their hollowed hum, to shape and render what has

become disembodied, for an instant, a blooming
a state of flux, scatters itself, like a new gesture
an unclenching that leans forward (tilts), as if looking
for lost kin. there it is, in a night, gone suddenly solid
to tell me of interior things. I thought I was woman
not animal, although here I am, wild and steaming—
not broken, nor thwarted, but standing in an open field
frosted grass crunching, beneath my hooves.

Nancy Shiffrin

Some Questions for Death

Death you old cliché in black hood and cape what are you doing here on my couch slouching legs
crossed foot tapping can't you wait and what were you doing in the hospital after Dad had his
heart attack and by-pass lurking in the halls visible only to me and what was his mother's ghost
doing at the foot of the bed shaking her head am I really the wrong daughter

where did I go in that spinning car I look down heart still beating though not so wildly as once
sky a cloudless leaky blue raucous sirens waking the city and up asking what to do with these
images neurons still singing the dream of diving for pearls comes back vivid threatening I still
can't write to the bottom of it

Death I know I can't beat you I only ask for a plan will it be 80 or 104 metaphor plagues me the
moon once associated with darkness dreams the feminine now understood as the rocky solid
which corrects the earth's wobbling tilt suddenly appears in daylight translucent disc in the
eastern sky

what is death or sleep or dreaming my soul goes to god and asks about that day at Vasquez Rocks
little girl flying from the cliffs brother mother grandfather and me barely able to breathe how the
child landed soft unbroken whole on this earth once thought to be flat stable now understood to
be blossoming with ever evolving life how many lives are enough

Two by Linda Singer

Convictions

I am a convict of
my own convictions
My truths hold me

captive to reactions
captive to confusion
captive to hope.

I am convinced life
is one consciousness,
one soul, one quest.

I think that energy
is trying to understand
itself through every single
one of our connections.

Maybe there is no right
or wrong.
Maybe there is only,
"That's interesting."

I believe in love, new
births, rebirths, tears,
holding, folding, coming,
going.

I believe in peanut butter,
Frappuccinos, pecan pie,
soy sauce, fried catfish,
avocados.

I believe in dreams,
hunches, past lives,

poems, novels, voices
in the night.

I believe in me,
and you and that
guy sitting alone
and that child crying
and that mother crying

and the individual who
feeds and hugs and cares for
them and then goes to the pound
and adopts an abandoned dog or cat
and then stops and lifts an earthworm
crawling across a blistering summer sidewalk.

I'll Be in My Room, Screaming

I'll be in my room, screaming.
I'm telling you this
because it will be
a silent scream,
with mouth
open,
dry.

It's a dream-scream,
only not a dream,
a sore throat
paranoia
sneeze
cough
curse

I pull shredded objects
from behind my tongue.
I can't swallow, can't
wash it down into
the acid bowl,
of my stomach,
to die.

Choking, in the clutch
of disease-anxiety
the fear of catching
the virus is the
deadliest
virus of
all.

Judith Skillman

The Grand Hotel

The tired mind can't conceive infinity.
I thought all night instead of sleeping, saw
dawn, walked out on the deck, watched rabbits snuffling.

Nest me, best me, better me, I'm agog, raw
with rubbing ideas—so many coach loads—
a googol, a googolplex of folks, in-laws

each to his or her own room. Experiment birds
sing like this awfully often, no?
Demonstrate this unimaginably weird

paradox, loosen the knot that ties me so
tightly, hardscrabble on my knees to such a
non-abundance, my take on aging. O how

dry, brittle, barren: a dream's insomnia.
Sheep countably wasted on the bland ceiling.
Titillation, when it comes, is heavy

laden, the bride groom has nothing—no, no ring.
Odd-numbered numbers riff between decimals.
I have not tasted that (space?) to which I take wing.

Coach loads arrive daily filled with guests' lawn-
colored luggage, these newbies disembark, fawn
over rooms pocket-doored, private, *and room for
one more?*--the call goes up from john to whore.

Two by Rick Smith

On Dad's Hundredth Birthday (2018)

You're hearing me, right?
I never know if you're listening.
Remember leaving Iowa City at 10?
We were already in jail in Lincoln by 2.
You were with me that day.
It took a damn helicopter
to track us.
We watched the Nebraska State Police
hang a U on Interstate 80
just to give us a ride
to the courthouse.

So April 19 would have been
your hundredth.
You've already been gone 30.

You said "I'll be going away
I'll be leaving you alone
to work things out
you came in alone
you go on alone"
and you handed me
"Leaves of Grass."

Dad, I've had the cuffs on me
more than that one time.
I've climbed into the front seat
of a limousine
to bicker over the price
of an 8-ball.
I was pulled out of La Bufadora
drunk and bleeding from stupidity.
Then, how bout that time in Herold Square

when Ballistics pulled two slugs
out of the door post an inch
from my head?
You were there.
We made The Daily News.

You're hearing me, right?
I'm never sure you're listening.

One time I had to sleep
at Penn Station
in February.
First, I had to walk there.
It was the only idea I had
that worked out that night.

And this was dumb:
I walked into Small's in Harlem
with some dude from West Virginia
to score.
I can't remember
how that one turned out

I'm an old man now
with grandchildren.
I'm a doctor, I live in the burbs.
I don't know if you're listening
or if you'd even recognize me.

I should have told this story
at your memorial:
we're driving home from N.Y.C.
on the backroads of Bucks County   > > >

> > > and a rabbit jumps out on the highway.
It was Brownsberg Road
and too late to brake.
It was just me and you
and that rabbit, still breathing.
We got home near midnight,
the rabbit wrapped in a towel,
trying to hold on.
You called the vet.
At the time, that seemed reasonable.
Now I know how weird it is
to call a vet at midnight
about a broken wild rabbit.
The vet said, "put him to sleep",
the injuries were too final.
You hooked up a hose to the exhaust pipe.
Then it was just you and me
in the Pennsylvania woods,
digging by lantern light.

They don't know this about you.
I know you hear me.

Donna Snyder

I will fear you and lie about it

Stay here with me,
your life a forfeit for my desire.
Feed me. Tell me what I need to hear.

But I still won't listen.
I'll kiss your presence only
when you are gone lonely and cold.
In the dark streets of my anger
I will fear you and lie about it,
unable to offer a consoling hand.

The Moments

Rising off a lake at early light,
at first I didn't recognize you there.
But somehow, in an afternoon,
we were in the same place
at the same time,
catching the right bus at a corner
in a different town.
Chance sat us together,
but there is no chance.
We talked all night
from Fontana to sun up.

Now, when the river passes,
we see the same paper boat,
the same wild flapping
of a heron rising,
the smooth depth charge
of a western grebe.
We see the visual,
then we hear the back beat.
It's all music,
it's suppose to happen,
it's happened before
and we're here for all of it.

I lock the door. Douse the light,
lying silent until I hear your clumsy trip.
And then I pounce. Anger in my eyes,

my ferocious aspect a spiked helmet.
I rub excreta in your face with an unlovely touch.

Your sorrow's ugliness justifies this torment.
The absence of compassion rips out my own heart.

Loren Kantor

HAPPY BIRTHDAY HANK BUKOWSKI 1920 - 2020!!

YOU OLD DOG!!

Woodblock print by Loren Kantor

T. Kilgore Splake

writing poetry

bukowski described chinaski's post office tenure
as slow death and murder, like my one time academic
college professorship, lifer sentenced to eternity of
8 a.m. lectures, endless bluebook scribblings, later
outpatient graduate, short term sanitarium "detox"
stay, going cold turkey with thorazine prescription,
drugstore shrinker, failing the marijuana "learned
experience," going back to booze, finally writing again
some poems knocking down small magazine space,

continuing to work, search for understanding
unlike younger "generation-xers complaining
of boredom, and nothing to do.

Jeanine Stevens

Coffee and Camels

I remember sounds like that from my childhood,
laughter for no cause, simply because the world is beautiful,
something like that.   Louise Glück

No, not the Sahara, but grandmother's
small kitchen in Appleton.

Woodstove in the center with percolator bubbling,
thick aroma of coffee and cigarettes
in gold packets showing Egyptian pyramids.

A family that enjoyed sitting,
talking and robust laughter.

Us kids sat watching, listening.
All seemed a stopping point to share.

On a Saturday, we would be sent
over the railroad tracks to the bakery
for crullers and schneckens (snails in German).

It wasn't so much what was said, but the genuine
attention given to each, no one rushed.

Later, it would be beer and polka, movement wild,
as the morning mood around this table was gentle.

It isn't so much that family fortunes are huge,
or what is left in trust…but models of patience
that are never forgotten.

On top the woodstove, an assortment of hand irons
lined up, warming to press Sunday clothes.

Lynn Tait

Bird Show Matinee at the Coffee Lodge

You've saddled me with a lie I never deserved.
You led me to believe I was responsible. – Irving Wallace, The Prize

She excuses herself,
dips into a script of anxieties,
pulls out last minute accusations,
dipsy doodles into a nest
of sticks and stones. Her big bird persona
deflects my home comfort sanity
for a coffee shop mugging.

I want to cut her delusions with a feather.

She tears into me, fluffed out and nasty,
squawking at imaginary shadows,
cracked up allegations a-flapping,
army of air behind her.
I'm projected as vulture in this bird show,
and feel the part like an allergy.
The doves have fled.

She sings like a canary desperate to peck everything to death.

I imagine mashing chocolate banana bread
like halved grapefruit Cagney style
into her phizog, her peek-a-boo hair,
or splattering her with cocoa a la Pollock painting.

Exit stage right rather than topple her fragile nest.
Wish I'd ordered sunflower seeds for the show,
iced coffee and road kill to go.

Two by G. Murray Thomas

DEMENTIA HAIKU

Hospital courtyard
Reflections in warped windows
dementia patients

Yellowed newspaper
Half-finished sudoku
Frozen lake

Mystified by the remote
Dad misses Lawrence Welk
Winter twilight

After our shopping trip
"Lost in the Supermarket"
my dad's new theme song.

Old memories
faded yellow photograph

Reflections shatter the scene
Memories come out
jumbled

Yesterday —
Glowing gold
and neon pink-orange
Today —
leaves all blown away

Landscape sketches
her artistic incarnation
buried in a notebook

She wants to go home.
But home is not a where,
it's a when.

FINGER LAKES HAIKU

One red tree among the green.
Too soon!

Took the wrong exit.
Wonderland of golden leaves
Getting lost reward.

Willow dangles
yellow teasers
of coming green.

Spring mud
Nourishes new growth
in the cemetery.

Hiking in the gloom
on an unfamiliar trail
Hidden waterfall

Thunder heads building
will there be lightning?
Hot date.

G. Murray Thomas

H. Lamar Thomas

Klimt In Color On The Banks Of The Tallulah River

Sanctus, Misère, Kaddish, Te Deum,
the flight was over,
the ground burned red behind a sheath of flowers,
everything was whispered Doloroso, Molto...
Guilty. Guilty by assimilation.
   Melt by fire.
Days come and go with songs of the Shulamite.
Sparkling cellophane crackle: thunderheads,
Tall as the sun this storm builds on near hillsides.
Come, break the heat...break damnit!
A different sunlight illuminates this flesh,
a procession of color, this pink,
freckled arm wrapped around a yoga waist,
hazel eyes accept my own green gaze;
and we talk about Ireland, Shanghai, and the South,
eat the same food and drink the same teas...
Summer rain. Lightening draws us closer.
Silver flash, sharp shadows,
a solarized moment, ozone snaps!
Are we guilty of forgetting?
forgetting funny difference
in the rush of weather and caress.
Desire prefers to forge on,
Metal and wood, air and water.
Necessity and need, want and have,
Because I do not sing Kol Nidre we are not the same,
but we share, we share these pastorals,
this street, these woods; this wide backed land
that sways to the beat of Whitman's Mississippi,
it holds us together. We speak the same language,
we share a culture, we are that culture,
we burn in August to the same sun.
History adds meaning,
but it is not meaning anything beyond this.
Can we drop difference for a day?

Bill Tremblay

ANIMATION

Sr. Monica comes out to the ballfield,
her white cowl arches like the Hollywood bowl.
I'm on my toes at third punching my glove,
ready for a hot grounder when I tell her
I'm going to see *Pinocchio.*
The talking cricket,
she announces, is a pagan spirit-demon, a liar
with a false conscience. I've seen the previews.
I'm going anyway. The house is so quiet
since my brothers and sister left I can hear
the neighbors twisting in their sheets.

Lights dim. Curtains part. A picture of
a clear night sky is different from stars sparkling
and dripping star-shine on a wood-carver's shop.
The cricket sings *When you wish upon a star ...*
so sweet how could it be false? Do I believe wishes
really can come true? A wish and a prayer: *quelle difference?*
He's had his doubts, but promises the story
that restored faith.
Gepetto puts his longing
for a son in every tap of his chisel. Out of the stars
a bubble descends gently carrying a Blue Lady
in a magic blue gown.
She gives the puppet speech.
He isn't a real boy yet. His smile is only painted on.
Gepetto dances with the answer to his prayers.
Coo-coo birds open their beaks and wail like Dixie.
A black kitten sashays and a goldfish with kissable lips
leaps and spins. Maybe this is a tale of temptation?
The clocks join in and the walls rock with joy.
Why isn't he a real boy?
The sun rises.
Children's laughter rings in the village streets.

His father and the kitten send him off to school.
The real temptation comes with Honest John
singing *Hey diddle-dee-dee ...*
Off they fly to Stromboli
at the puppet circus. He dances and the audience
throws gold. *You've had your fun, now you must pay!*
says the human volcano. He locks the wooden boy
in a cage without supper. What does he care?
He's made of wood.

It'll take a miracle for us to get out of this,
says Jiminy Cricket. The Blue Fairy again
sails down to set Pinocchio free. Pinocchio isn't
really bad like the Fox who puts him on a stage coach
bound for Pleasure Isle. Pinocchio gets a donkey
ear for every cigar he smokes. A radiant pigeon
rises from the sea with a scroll in its beak.
*Gepetto went looking for you and got swallowed
by Monstro the whale.*
A family reunion inside
the whale with hugging and dancing. I wish for
a bright idea to bring my family together again
like Pinochio made the whale sneeze.
From dark theater to dark streets

I walk in a light rain wishing for a Blue Lady
to change my legs from wood to flesh.

My brothers and sister sleep in my body like dolls.
I am their orphan. I look down at my shoes,
shake my head like a buffalo calf. What is Sr. Monica's
beef against Mr. Disney? That he can make an animated
miracle where the lost at last come home,
and he isn't even ordained?

Two by William Mohr

THE SUNDERING

This afternoon I foresaw my deathbed wish:
The northern and southern hemispheres
Of a radish, placed one after the other
On my tongue, each salted so the juice
Of being bitten down upon dissolves
in creek-beds of disbelieving joy.

AMARYLLIS

My daughter would be named
for you, if I had one;
so let the luscious anthem
of these brusque red trumpets
resound for other daughters,
other sisters! Even as this trio
of blossoms shrivels and wilts,
may your procession of
dormant bulbs engorge
this slowly hardening soil.

Maja Trochimczyk

This Afternoon

You are the music while the music lasts.
        ~ T.S. Eliot, Little Gidding

The woodpecker measures time by the thickness
of tree trunks. Birds make nests, hidden from
hawks, safe from scrub jays. We wake in sunlight,
with twirling patterns still under our closed eyelids.

We listen to high-pitched calls of hummingbirds,
the random flutter of wings. We breathe in spring air
with smoothly flowing melodies of birdsong,
the sweetest of nectars. Waves crash on distant shores
of the Pacific. Stars appear dimly above the horizon,
that glows with the bronzed orange of departing Sun.

We live on the planet of children's laughter.
We watch refractions of light in my sapphire ring,
on diamond dew drops that cling to blades of grass,
half-opened roses. We live on Earth of abundance
and beauty. We live on Earth of plenitude and calm.

There are no sorrows here, no worries.
No before, nor after. No plans. We take deep
breaths, count to eight, inhaling smiles to the tips
of our fingers, into our toes. I laugh. You laugh.
Crystalline peals echo through the Universe –
from galaxy to galaxy, star to star.

We grow and grow – infinite, gentler, wiser –
we understand all, embrace all, know all.
Perfection. Presence. Light.

        Originally from Rose Always - A Love Story (rev. 2020)

Lauren Tyler

DON'T READ THIS POEM

—if you want to learn life,
take what Caesar gave you and use it:
buy a young tree. For beginners,
choose something deciduous,
something that will flower
and bear fruit in the fullness of time.
Plant the sapling carefully:
you are a steward to it,
but it does not belong to you.

Look at it each morning, very closely,
this dead, twisted stick that came in the mail,
or that you chose from a pile of kindling
at the nursery, with a bag of sawdust
packed 'round the ugly tangle of bare roots
more like rotten rope than anything alive.

Notice when the winter-dormant wood
quickens, knuckles-up—watch these blistered nubs:
they will become branches, buds, leaves.
Notice how the texture and color of a new leaf
changes as it grows and matures,
watch the elegant patterns of branching emerge.
Look at other, bigger trees—study
how their patterns differ, now that you can see them.
And in the second year, or the fourth,
the tree's winter skeleton
may surprise you with blossoms,
tissue-paper soft, vibrant against dark wood.

The quiet hours of early morning are good for this.
Look also in the sideways light of evening—
you can spare that much time,
and you should: do that, every day. Don't read this:
do that, for years. Then think back:
the handful of hours spent sweating
with soaker and shovel
under the skirt of the sky,
will have taught you more, and better,
than a small heap of words like this.
And the tree can give you fruit.

Vachine

Sister Sonnet

She lost a young daughter in a Drive-by.
Doesn't mean left in a hard-to-find place,
see, lost means her girl was shot dead.
Strangers in a C-MBZ owned outright
by that Candyman out on the Central,
a deuce of Crip Heats cruising kinda
thought hers was a Blue house, rubbed
a 9, slipping by, 'cuza Blood's dues, yo.
Mama, just raising children there, heads
just above the Man's water-line wages.
No slack given, none asked. Hope, dirty
word thereabouts, her eyes down skipping
sidewalk cracks, not breaking Mama's back,
her wails don't even reach County morgue.

Two by Katharine VanDewark

Dust from Mongolia

Apparently, early spring winds sweep
dust from the Mongolian plains
all the way across China
to and beyond Beijing.
I know this because a friend said so.

Millions of people anticipate the
coming wind and chant
as with the Indian monsoon –
"When the rains come".
"When the dust comes."
This has been happening for centuries.
Or at least for years.

How has the grass been uprooted
that soil is picked up easily and
blown for miles?
Are nomads to blame?
Was it the conquering hoards of
Genghis Khan and his horses
that trampled the carpets to dirt and
started the whole thing?

Did they pulverize the blades
playing polo across the steppes using the
decapitated heads of prisoners as balls?

When the grass grew back
and dew collected on it
was it red?

Was it the weight of yurt floors
that compacted it and caused it to die
of asphyxiation?

Or was it a
lack of oil poured into the earth
to grease the hinges of vengeance gods?

Short Poems: Not Tanka or Haiku But….. Tanku!

1.
I packed boxes all day
folding my life into cardboard.
I look at my bedroom
bare without books and
items on my dresser and wonder
        if I like it better this way.

2.
Someone drops a knife
on the black and white
square tile floor. It
sounds like my heart
        that stops in bed at night.

3.
A garden watercolor it's
deckled edge floating
in a window mat.
Underneath
my headless chest
        reflected in a narrow mirror.

4.
On my left wrist I wear a
gold watch and
bracelet linked with
enameled shields. Outside
the night is full of rain
        wind and cold air.

5.
I complain about small things:
bad grammar
yellow socks
a bad back.
Never mentioning
        what keeps my awake each night.

6.
In a white bistro
bowl, open mussels
steam, green flecks of
parsley litter the rim.
Under the table my feet
        sweat in yellow rain boots.

7.
He likes me in dresses
"Oh, you're dressed up today,"
he says. I wonder
about my rage under
        this silk blouse and linen skirt.

8.
I stay in all morning
working on my taxes.
It's raining outside and
I stare at the ocean
huge waves pounding
        a barren beach.

9.
I have a blockage that
affects my inner ear and
gives me an excuse to
        misunderstand what you say.

10.
After three years of
marriage she still didn't
understand his handwriting.
Following the divorce
        she got every word.

Richard Vidan

JUST SOME OF THE THINGS
THAT COULD KILL YOU
(IN ALPHABETICAL ORDER)

Adventure. Alcohol. Ambition. Andiron. Anthrax.
Bacon. Banality. Bear. Boomerang. Boredom. Botulism.
Cancer. Capitalism. Car. Communism. Covid 19. Cudgel.
Dart. Delusion. Dentistry. Disease. Domesticity.
Earthquake. Egotism. Ennui. Envy. Excitement.
Faith. Fame. Fear. Fire. Flood. Friend.
Gas. Genocide. Grandiosity. Greed. Gun.
Hate. Heroin. Hippo. Hope. Hubris. Husband.
Ignorance. Impulse. Indigence. Inertia.

Raindog

Jaguar. Jail. Jaundice. Javelin. Justice.
Ketamine. Kindness. Knife. Knowledge.
Laser. Lethargy. Loneliness. Love. Lust.
Malice. Medication. Mendacity. Misogyny.
Nazi. Nightshade. Nitroglycerin. Normality.
Obesity. Openness. Opium. Opprobrium.
Petulance. Politics. Pomposity. Potion.
Quicksand. Quicksilver. Quiescence.
Racism. Radiation. Religion. Revenge. Riches.
Sadness. Sex. Stroke. Stupidity. Suicide. Surgery.
Talent. Tiger. Tornado. Torture. Toxin.
Umbrage. Unsanitariness. Uranium.
Venom. Veracity. Violence. Vitriol.
War. Weather. Wife. Worry. Wrath.
Xenophobia. X-rays. Xylophonist (insane).
Yahoos. Yak. Yearning. Yoyo.
Zamboni. Zealot. Zebra.

Two by Ted Washington

Symbiosis

I can't let go of you. You won't let me. How did it come to this?

I should be thankful for the push. You thought you were done with me, but you can't push that hard — or didn't.

You wanted distance. I learned that I needn't be that close; two drones on rotation for uninterrupted observation.

Micro-mini cameras hidden for surveillance. Your room. Your bath. Your car. Your workplace. The will be no chance of escape.

The airwaves connect us now. My nourishing fix available twenty-four-seven. Wi-fi enabled and uploaded live, my reach is global.

You are becoming an internet sensation, virtually viral. Dedication sites create unverified profiles, unreliable wiki. IP'd someone on constant feed.

It turns out I'm the tool. My obsession is your obsession. Your router on endless stream. You sit before the screen watching you, watching you.

Jungle

He longed for some different world, some unknown place more primitive than this mechanized, computerized society. Byron hated his job. Why did he have to be the bad guy? He searched for a stick. Stall 27B, expired; the handheld printer dispensed the ticket. He placed it under the wiper. Here we go, Byron picked up the stick. Once an angry lady ran over his foot. Didn't they know if the timer said time's up, there was nothing he could do. The dead pigeon was animated by the horde of ants. He poked it, the stick was quickly engulfed. Vicious.

Two by Lawrence Welsh

NEW MEXICO GHOST TOWNS

one becomes another now
that's hammered to dust
and in the only window left
of the texaco gas station
an image or visage to disappear
and appear again:

once for copper
once for oil
once for marijuana
once for cotton and chile

they become worthy of nothing:
just old neon and rust
and the wind
        pointing that way

AFTER GIVE 'EM ENOUGH ROPE

a hanging over sand
or crucifixion face down to flip
in cruciform for face up
as eyes see only sun:
the blindness of all sight
the explosions of color
and then the ecstasies
only the vultures may see

Jeffrey Alfier

Lyn White

Giants

It takes a giant
to take hold
of the sun
and wrap it up
like a lantern
and hold it
there shining gold.
There were such giants once,
so it is said.
They would light the way of travelers,
guide them through the darkness
and shine a light for all of us,
guide our way,
so it is said.
It is said that
we killed them all.
Even though it is difficult to kill a giant.
We worked out ways to do it,
worked out ways to kill
them all.
So now we just have only the sun
and now it shines less than before.
Now
we have no giants
to capture it
and wrap it up
like a lantern.
Now
we have no lantern
to guide us through
the darkness
anymore.

First published in With
Painted Words, March 2018

Charles Wilkinson

Underwriting

Antonym of purple
would have you plain, Style:
each point of policy
nailed to the page, & the whole text
limpid as dew
or these pebbles and shining fish
seen through a glass
that brings them nearer to the eye;
the stile in the fence
entices towards a field, ambiguous
even in the day:
the path not shown, the hills grey bruises
beneath the skin;
this distance is the true whiteness of the way,
your walking with risk;
what writes under this mist is present:
no cloud-pothole's
unsteady trick. In wisps of words
we claim the light -
& lovely turbulence we cannot see;
it gives us no slip
& and will not lie, stay for signature,
assure, indemnify:
provide with coverage against the night.

Pamela Williams

Palm Reading

I can't help but think first of
Fauci's face palm, subtle as it was.
Seeming attempt to squelch laughter at
the absurdity of the Cirque that
this has become. Lunacy, greed,
subterfuge run rampant.
Rampant, the descriptor for our
times. The endless and futile quest
to accurately narrate this
twilight zone. Would it offer ablution,
I wonder, to just put down all those
marvelous adjectives on a page,
for posterity? Like the cleansing,
purging aspect of morning pages?

And the determination of my planting.
Knowing the inevitable companion lessons.
Visualizing healing flow with vigilant watering.
This year, herbs and vegetables. Searching
for some measure of my own sovereignty?

I keep plodding up my rocky hill,
certain of the curative value in ascent.
Necessity for both dog and me.
Reveling each time in the rewarding vistas,
grace in this remote and reflective place.

This week, in an offering to serenity, or closure,
or acceptance, I guess, I took some ashes to scatter,
from the precipice of that rock face you so
triumphantly scaled. My own cathartic progress,
my palm infused with yours.

Jay Blommer

Redacted poem #2

The world is full of strangers.

, wandering
through the ghostly tendrils

of

the weak heart

Jay Blommer

Kelsey Bryan-Zwick

Speaking Ill

Sometimes, mid-sentence even, I stop
a breath short from mentioning my sister
who died.

Because in the awkward paused space
someone eventually tries to fill this silence
with a condolence, *Deepest sympathies,*
with the question

How did she die?

And I don't want to lie, I want to scream
I don't want to say. Like the rest of us
one day, she stopped breathing

Breathing. That's all she could do
near the end. And that only with
the help of machines.

I don't want to say we had to decide
one day to unplug those machines, to stop
the pumps keeping her alive.

I don't want to say
I want to scream
the words fall from
my face like stones
Cirrhosis of the liver

She had some health problems
those final few years she was always
in and out of the emergency room

I didn't go to visit
that last time at the hospital
before leaving to go back to college
it felt like suffocating, sitting there
watching her wounds

Alcoholism mostly. And pills.
There had been a bad weight loss surgery
that changed how her liver processed things,
or didn't—but she knew she had to stop drinking
and she couldn't, didn't, though it was
little sip, *Only little slips*, she'd insist
Just one celebratory glass of wine

I don't want to say how I had to clean
out her room, the stashes and stashes
of pills I found, prescribed bottles
I threw out one by one with bare and
grieving hands

I don't want to say. I want to scream
I don't want you to think it was her fault
she was so sick, not even the doctors could
cure her.

Officially Sealed: collage by Patti Sullivan

ESSAYS & MICRO-FICTION

April Bulmer

THE FAITH HEALER

I ACHE from head to toe. My arches have fallen. I wear heavy black shoes to support my feet. My mind is low today like a morning moon. Perhaps it will rise in the dim, though my faith in God has waned. The energy healer is slim and young. He has high cheek bones and a narrow face. I think he is Jewish, like me. His woman, too. She wears her hair long and sports thick black glasses. She is expecting. There are two other people here. A woman who suffers back pain and an old man who bears his weight on a cane. The man fires questions at the couple. I am a lawyer, he says. Can you heal cancer?...Is this an exorcism? he shouts and hobbles away. The woman stands before the healer. My name is Zach, he says to her. As an advanced-level energy worker, I can heal you in a session. I will address the root cause of your disorder and align your energetic body. Unbalanced energy centers itself in us, often in the root chakra. It can lead to immune issues and diseases. We only mask the symptoms with medications and supplements, he says. "I can heal your body at the very source of the disease." Zach is lithe as he moves around the woman. He does not touch her, or lay his hands upon her, but beats against the field that surrounds her. His gestures are large and wild at times. I was first aware of the gift when I was three years old, he says. Later, I helped my brother, who suffers from schizophrenia, to manage the symptoms of his mental illness. The woman shakes her head and massages her back. She waves him a big goodbye. He kneels before me and pushes at an energy he admits he can't see. I feel a light breeze as he moves around my crippled body. He looks pale and tired as he finishes his last assault at what ails me. He heaves a big sigh. I feel as though I was just hit by a Mack Truck, he says. His woman hands him a bottle of water. She rubs her belly. I think of *ruach elohim*, as I drive home in the February wind, the breath of God moving over the deep.

Out of Darkness, Light
Poems By April Bulmer

Hidden Brook Press –
John B. Lee Signature Series

$21.95 (Includes Shipping)
april.poet@bell.net

"Individual voices of this fictional congregation speak to the absolute bone and blood of love and sacrifice... There is worship here that opens body as well as spirit..."

Katherine L. Gordon

Coco

THE MAKING OF THE COMMON BOOK, VOL. 74

MY FIRST companion, my first love, my closest friends were all books. I didn't have a normal childhood, but what is normal nowadays anyway? I grew up in and out of the hospital. From the toddling age of terrible two, I was hooked up to an IV and secluded from the world in my hospital bed room. For two years, I lived there. In a hospital room; changing nurses, replacing IV bags,

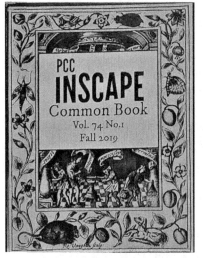

I watch my world come and go from my bed. No one ever stayed to play. Just me, a room full of books, puzzles and my Rainbow dog. I still have that dog, and in my memories, he was bigger than Clifford. Sitting in the corner of my room, stained, lackluster, faded colors of youth; his orange now a pale cream-scicle, ears and paws once vibrant now faded rainbows covered in smog colored dirt. Rainbow Dog stares into the nothing, a small frail puppy size stuffed animal.

The only constant in my life were books. Books with pictures, and without. Books with covers that changed as often as the people who wandered in and out of my room. Books became the only thing I could count on, trust in, feel safe with. Books were my guiding light. I was always fascinated, wide eyed, and full of life when I knew a new book was coming.

Flash to present day, we got the opportunity to watch a book be made. The sites and sounds of the paper room felt like home. I could smell the different pages, delight in ink stained fingers, marvel at the universe of creation. I felt like Charlie in Willy Wonka's factory.

No one would ever suspect the torment I was in just moments before class. I document these painful day to day transgressions through photographs. A visual diary if you will. Reminders that I made it past the enemy lines of mental warfare once again.

I couldn't pass up the opportunity to watch the creation of literary life born before my very eyes. Standing outside the library conference room after the battle I snap a picture of what it's like to suffer with mental illness. I had just attended a panel conducted by an outside company on how to effectively support people like me. It was all for naught in the end when I was placed in the center of ridicule and shame. A martyr for what truly happens when most are exposed to people like me.

I would not let my madding thoughts take hold of me. Take a selfie and move on - physically to a scholars journey of empowerment. Wiping away tears and tying back my hair I enter the printing room and join the rest of the INSCAPE crew. See everything is okay! My thoughts as I take another selfie, this time in the printing room with the staff in the background. I can see it in my own eyes that I'm not ok.

That printed and embossed smile, a boldfaced lie. I find it ironic that the issue we are printing is an alchemist common book. There is magic and transformation that awaits me in this issue. But, will I ever find the spell, the elixir, or formula that will rid my torment? Standing in this Dr. Jekyll facade doing my best to keep my Hyde in superfluous, strepitous, subconscious thought. Serpentine thoughts slither boisterously, as coiled anxiety thrust its venomous attack. I need this distraction to focus on anything other than anguish.

I watch copies of the book being spit out like 9mm rounds out of a gun. This Canon Color C8000VP is an arsenal of literary ammunition. So many different printable materials, card-stock, parchment, glossy and non-glossy, magazine, poster board, banners here I stood in my Louvre marveling at all the art. Listening to the humming music of pages in print. Within less than minutes there on the output tray were 5 fresh copies of the Common Book. Pages that felt like satin and glistened like river water at dawn under the soft lights of the room. Such a magical experience, I glide my index finger up and down the page like an ice skater on fresh ice. My eyes fixated on the rich color and intricate details that show without so much as a smudge or pixilation of any kind. A portrait from 1582 looks back at me and there it is! That time portal that allows me to travel around the world and throughout time while standing perfectly still. This...this is salvation and freedom in its purest form, a transcendent enchantment.

The journey continues, for to be born isn't enough clean up and dressing is needed. From copier to BLM booklet maker the next surgical process begins. Wire stitching reminds me of staples that once held my flesh together after the birth of my two children now fastens and binds the contents of this newborn book. I've lost count of how many surgeries, and many IV markings, stitches and staples that have held me together over the years. I touch my tracheotomy, adjust my necklace, I know this feeling of being held together, but still able to come apart. I know this feeling day in and day out with anxiety and depression that pulls at my seems threatening to tear me apart.

The Sorcerer delicately holds up an almost finished copy with his spiritualistic fingers. How many worlds has he created? How many marveled printed enchantments has he cast? Crew members study carefully with bewilderment and bare witness to Frankenstein like sutures wondering what is the last step that completes this evolution of life.

This last step is a crucial and precise. It requires mastery, patience, skilled practiced expertise. The amount of precision that is needed will be paramount to the final blessing of creation. Here in this scriptoria like room we await mens et manus (hand and mind) made elegance. Only these magicians hold the secrets to the perfect elements and technique to conjure up these immortal gifts of life.

It's time...the "final cut" so to speak. Placed within the "Guillotine" perfectly measured, tactfully placed upon the altar, fitted with meticulous care unfit scraps of no longer needed empty space will be removed. Swift as a scalpel through flesh paper is severed and discarded like an amputated umbilical cord. Flashes of how many pieces of myself have been severed from me over the years. Wasted, infected, unneeded, defective, outside the lines of worth removed scraps got tossed in the waste bin.

What do I share in common with this book? Everything...

Joseph Farley
AT THE STATION

A MAN in a suit and a bowler hat stands on the train platform reading the Financial Times. He seems oblivious to all but stocks and futures, and you, the only other person there, ignore him.

You hear the train approaching, and turn to watch it pull into the station. Suddenly you feel a powerful kick propelling you towards the tracks and probable death. At the last moment, you regain your balance, surviving, just barely. You turn around to stare at the bastard, but he pretends not to see you.

He calmly folds his paper, and boards the train, standing in the doorway so you cannot get on. He tips his hat as the doors close in your face and the train pulls out, leaving you behind with your anger.

It is only after the train has gone that you realize the man has taken your wallet, and, somehow, your shoes as well. You do not know just what to make of this, and know even less when the police arrest you for reporting the crime.

"Something has changed in this world," you tell yourself, as the chains are set to wrists and ankles.

You are thrust into the hold of a galley and ordered to row. While the lash licks your back, you see your nemesis from the station up on deck sipping cocktails with his friends.

The captain says, "We have finally gotten this vessel headed in the right direction."

"Here, Here," chants a chorus of bankers and fund managers.

You look carefully, see one of them is wearing your shoes.

The whip cracks, and you pull harder. What else can you do?

"It's the economics stupid." Someone shouts in your ear.

You try hard to understand, but are soon too exhausted to think beyond the next day.

Your bench-mate is a true believer. He whispers, nodding towards the man with martini, "We'll get there too if we work hard enough."

You wonder about that.

Next thing you know it's raining. You look up, shaking the drops from your head, and see the suits zipping up, no umbrellas in their smiles.

Jesse James Kennedy

THE SUBURBS

YOU SEE the pimp in the ghetto who preys on young girls and you shake your head. But you smile at Cindy the pretty sixteen-year-old cheerleader down the street and her family. You don't know about the scars on her ankle that she cuts into her own flesh with a razor blade because the pain is the only thing that can make her stop thinking about what her step-dad is going to do when he sneaks into her room that night after her mom's sleeping pills kick in. You know that any of those urban street kids could be packing a gun and may kill their peers at any moment. They are thugs, it's that simple. But Tommy, that nice, quiet young man who cuts your grass. You don't know about how he looks at the pistols in his dad's gun cabinet every chance he gets and how he tries to find the courage to do it tomorrow. And when the hate finally drowns out the last bit of hope and he takes that pistol to school and finally finds peace by letting out that hate in a blizzard of bullets before turning it on himself and escaping the only way he thinks he can, no one will call the little demons that used to shove his head in the toilet at school thugs nor will they call him one. Instead, they will talk about the tragedy of being mentally ill. You see the heroin addicts overdosing in the alley ways of inner cities and just figure that's what they get for choosing that life. But when Linda, the kind but tired looking housewife who always buys your kid's girl scout cookies, finally takes too many Xanax with her vodka martini and doesn't wake up in the morning, it will just be called heart-failure, and you'll pray for her family. Welcome to the suburbs, where you can walk safely down the street because the monsters are camouflaged behind sprawling lawns, white fences and beautiful two-story homes, the well-dressed rapists will smile and wave, and the tragedies of desperate people won't disturb you, because the victims have the decency to cry alone at night behind closed doors and only scream inside their own tortured minds. America's Shangri-La where happiness is built on denial and illusion.

KICKING TOWARDS THE DEEP END
Lisa Segal

(available on Amazon)

"Lisa Segal dips her toes into the deep end of her private history in these bittersweet poems. Alternately sensual and arid, comic and grief-stricken, *Kicking Towardz the Deep End* dances with time and place in this unique, unforgettable collection."

Alexis Rhone Fancher, author of *Junkie Wife* and *The Dead Kid Poems*. Poetry editor, *Cultural Weekly*

Marie Lecrivain

WHAT IF MARIA GORRETI WANTED ACCESS TO BIRTH CONTROL?

YOU COULD be an 80's girl growing up in a small town like Mentone, Alabama, or 1980's Santa Clarita, California. You're the oldest, and the only daughter, whose mom works two jobs. She has no time to spend with you, other than a quick kiss on your cheek, as she leaves for work in the morning, or a murmured "thanks" for making sure your brothers finished their math homework. The first signs of adolescence are upon you; slender hips round into curves, and the occasional zit on your forehead. The neighbor boy spies on you from his bedroom window.

You're aware of your desirability. TV informs you, with ads and after school specials, about teen sex, and Jordache Jeans, which you'll never be able to afford on your mom's salary. The older girls at school daily brag about making it to second base, getting fingered, or going all the way.

When will it be your turn? Part of you wants to give in, but you're a good catholic girl who goes to confession on Saturdays, and church on Sundays. You know premarital sex is a sin. It'll destroy your virtue, and turn you into a scarlet woman with an M tattooed on your chest. You don't want to end up like your mother; married at 17, mother at 18, and finally, a burned out divorcee at 28.

You struggle to balance hormones against dogma, and seek peace in stories about Agnes with the long hair, Lucy with her eyeballs on a platter, and Dymphna with her sword and crown. One evening, you raid your mother's medicine cabinet for some aspirin, and find a stash of condoms on the top shelf.

What will you do, Maria?
What will you do?

BINARY PLANET

Poems by Henry Crawford

"Henry Crawford's book will be one of your favorites this year"

Grace Cavalieri, Maryland Poet Laureate

"Another wonderful collection from this fine, American poet."

RD Armstrong, Publisher

The Word Works
www.TheBinaryPlanet.com

John Macker
TONY MOFFEIT'S "RATTLESNAKE MOJO"

*"and what do you call it? you call it outlaw.
and what do you call it? you call it ghost lan-
guage. because it is a phantom. and because it
is blood. ghostblood billy. billy the kid. because
he reached the intensity of himself."*
—Tony Moffeit

I'VE KNOWN poet Tony Moffeit since the early 1980's, in Denver, when we'd run across one another at readings or other gatherings. We were both finding our way as writers at the time, and I, for one, had a young voice that was raw, rough, trying to get at real. One of the first times I heard him up close was at some third floor converted minimalist red brick Kerouac-esque warehouse space in downtown Denver, a new loft-type interior, suitable for performance. I was wondering who this cat was, from Pueblo, Colorado, dressed in shiny black leather, accompanying himself on the bongos like some incantatory, skinny white shadow. He had his voice down and it was a good sound. I remember walking away perplexed. I didn't know what he was up to exactly or where he was going with it. I knew for sure, though, he believed what he was doing. While the rest of us were learning to emote cool, Tony was blowing, scatting, chanting, rhyming hot. It was coming from some deep subterranean spirit place where the blues get form and climb up the burning urgency of the voice straight up to the street. I quickly got the Pentecostal suggestion of his rhythms: this man could sing. He conjured Ray Charles,

he conjured Mick Jagger . . but with poetry! You could hear volcanic traces of San Francisco poet/street singer Jack Micheline, or New Mexico's Kell Robertson; traces of Kerouac's *Mexico City Blues.*

Tony isn't really Beat, he doesn't come from the Eastern Establishment, or Black Mountain or Language poetry. He doesn't have much to do with the Boulder- Naropa poetry folks necessarily.

I found out later he'd invented (or divined) "outlaw poetry" with Albuquerque poet Todd Moore, of *Dillinger* fame. As Tony once said, "When I think of outlaw, I think of a change in consciousness, a new level of consciousness. The first outlaws, to me, were those who initiated a change in thinking, a change in living, a change in viewpoint. Turning the world upside down."

Tony also writes a tender, but unsentimental ballad; and the short poem as well, succinct, direct, full of emotion. I have a copy of his 2000 book, *billy the kid & frida kahlo*: on one level an expansion or re-imaging of Michael McClure's classic 1968 chapbook, *The Sermons of Jean Harlow & The Curses of Billy the Kid*, but the execution is all Moffeit's, 2 historically flawed characters riffing on the endless possibilities of love and violence. Billy's myth is huge, it'll take more than one poet to disassemble it. As Todd Moore once wrote in a dispatch from Dodge City where they were featured in an outlaw poetry summit of sorts: "Tony Moffeit is singing . . all new songs and they are almost like a mixture of honky tonk wise guy and the big dark elegy blues, they are restrained and sad, and have a big hint of duende in them . . ."

His poem, "I'll never get out of this night alive" is a 3 paragraph Indian death chant without punctuation, an incantatory rant celebrating the absolute primal ecstasy of writing without borders, without intrusions, throughout the night, minus the soul's revision, taking a wild last breath ride with the devil across the terrain of absolute solstice blackness called the poem:

"i talk with ghosts i am mad i admit that but it is in my madness that i see most clearly the purest outlaw act is that of mad love but how can I explain that which can only be grasped in a phrase a syllable a fleeting feeling maybe an old blues from the radio in the wee hours of the morning or the voice from a telephone an outlaw voice a renegade voice a desperado feeling out of the blackness of the empty room . . ."

Likewise, in this passage from "Outlaw Blues", he sings,

" . . tonight i sing a blues song for the outlaws the renegades the desperados who drift under endless skies america your clouds are my songs your rain is my voice your hail is my blues."

I've always admired how Tony's poems breathe freely, how they bask in the white heat of their own rhythms and rebelliousness; no capitals, very little punctuation save for the breath line, his poems begin without fanfare or pretense, they are songs that occur in the middle of life, in the middle of language, in the moment, like all of our dreams do, distilled down by his considerable craft into moments that bear witness, that bear the burden and primal joy of the spoken blues. They don't have a beginning, middle or an end in the formal sense. Each poem seems to embrace its own mythology, its own urgency, its own desperado society of rhythms and this is what gives his poems their form. Yes, they can be certainly elegiac, a funereal progression of words lamenting a gone era or hero, but they are also full of their own subversive energy suggesting that these heroes, these feelings, these rhythms that manifest themselves in Tony's unique performances on and off the page, will live on.

His short poem "Sid and Nancy" from his 2011 book, *Born to be Blue,* is a matter-of-fact, slightly chilling document loosely based on the last days of the short-lived love of 2 punk icons with 2 feet in their graves: "love was strung through the eye of a needle"/ ". . . and chaos was cruising in a black limousine/their invisible children in the abyss of words/imprisoned and set free on the highway/even their luggage was alive." The last line is Moffeit's surreal, cold-eyed tribute to those doomed few destined to live and die forever in the penumbrae: "the mirrors were cracking all by themselves."

He's speaking of course, for the Charlie Starkweather's and Carol Fugate's of the world, the Bonnie Parker's and Clyde Barrow's, the disaffected and desperate, bludgeoned into infamy by the wreckage of the American dream. Tony knows these souls. His poetry travels by night. It can be heard in the crackling car radio static at midnight in the middle of oblivion Kansas. It can be heard in Woody Guthrie's song "Deportee (Plane Wreck at Los Gatos) or "Pancho and Lefty" by Townes Van Zandt. Or any song by Hank Williams. (Tony's fine short poem to Hank can be found in the summer 2010 issue of *Malpais Review: " . .how did it feel at the end of the universe/when all the mirrors in the universe had gone blind and/you couldn't even find the slurred syllables/of your broken hearted songs and you/ were stranded in the middle of the night."*) It can be heard in the distinctly American rhythms of speech of the noir films of the late 1940's and 50's.You can sense the almost familial attraction and anarchic romanticism echoing in Moffeit's words.

Sometimes I think Tony went down to the Crossroads to sell his soul to the devil for poetry. Sometimes, when I watch him perform live, I think the hellhound is on his trail. Most of the time, though, I think Tony is just merrily possessed by poetry in all of its incarnations. He's aware of the singular (and intellectual) rebelliousness of characters as disparate as Nietzche and Boddhidharma, and to Tony, they effortlessly wear the imprimatur of the outlaw. Acknowledging this bloodline, he's aware of the lyrical hell-raising of Charles Bukowski, Robert Johnson and even Diane DiPrima as important influences, as well. (Di Prima's Loba cycle I think qualifies for outlaw masterpiece status.) Tony is not only adept at provoking this wayward, grieving spirituality from the blues or "street language", he can make you feel it without sentimentality. His work is generous and not obscure, it lets you into its world without having to show your photo ID.

Tony once wrote, "Like the shaman, the outlaw is interested in the secret energies of the universe."

"Tony Moffeit has always lived at the edge of his nervous system. He howls his poems in performance and he writes poetry doing 80 on Route 25. His is a high speed America and his dreams are energized with Duende and blood."
—Todd Moore

Closer to home, in *Born to be Blue*, Tony writes of "the camposantos the decorated graves of New Mexico" in the poem "Saeta" after a Miles Davis composition. Tony conjures a witch's brew of murder on a warm night, listening to jazz in his town of Pueblo, how "the war is on my doorstep", how sudden death enters his now vulnerable neighborhood psyche:
> "there are no camposantos no roadside
>   graves for

Attention Memoirists
Take the stress out of writing your or a family member's life legacy story. Let me do the work for you through a series of interviews.
505-603-5930
artqueen58@aol.com

> two priests who were slain in their rectory
>   no pink
> carnations no red and yellow roses no
>   wooden crosses
> only the flaming horn of miles davis piercing the night
> like a blade ablaze turning the violence to
>   love turning
> the pain to passion sweeping the darkness
>   into the
> spectacle of autumn that precedes rebirth."

A perfect elegiac jazz/Zen rebuttal to the sudden violence that can happen anywhere, but especially on a warm pueblo night when the poet is writing against its terrible roar and attempting to redeem it from its horror. Tony realizes that it is the poet, like the shaman, who must conjure a new light from the darkness and it is called peace:
> tonight two priests were slain across the
>   street and i
> can feel them in this solo fever in the
>   blood this
> never giving up this obsession for more
>   life for more love
> challenging the chaos of the killer's lust to
>   rage for the
> power of the silence and the power of the
>   word to rage
> against hate to rage against death to rage
>   for the song

to rage for the art to rage for the passion
    of lovers
and the passion of poets alone solitary
    singers all the
warriors of living breathing energy force
    power
warriors of peace

Moffeit's unique sense of proportion, rhythm and passion transforms a series of sentences not just into a plaintive chant for peace and love but into a propulsive nocturne which shape-shifts tragedy into redemptive words of hope.

He writes as though it's his duty *and* his muse.

In "as it is as it was as it will be", also in *Born to be Blue*, the reader will find the caldera where many of Tony's poetic (and performance) concerns live and breathe. In this poem, he turns the blues chant and its accompanying duende, inward; he's got his "rattlesnake mojo" working from the inside out, on "the smells from the streets of mexican food and gasoline," but he's a poet with no name, no identity, a recording instrument, "reduced to zero", he sleeps on the wind, dreams poems, shakes the rattlesnake with "a wild born mojo" and the second half of the poem gains an epic, organic momentum:

" . . take some dust and roar
traveling down
those ghost tracks
that train whistle
those bones under the ground
singing the blues of the earth
fingers on skin
the rooster crows all day in the alley
as it is as it was as it will be
miracles and nothing less
time waiting on a streetcorner
holsters dancing with guns
boots dancing with feet
in a mexican hotel
every yesterday becomes tomorrow
time conquered in the alien dust of abandon

of a fastdraw moon
locomotive unleashed on abandoned
    tracks
anguish of loco wind
i want to wear your eyes
i want the rainbow to be paralyzed
i want to live in a town without a name
the then that is now
the now that is then
when motion becomes space
destination unknown
talking stalking
to finally get down to it

billy the kid & frida kahlo is a sequence of poems which takes place between these two bruised, iconic characters, in the supposed middle of their rather short lives. Each poem is quiet, but crackling with mortality. They are not as much a communication or Socratic dialogue between the two as much as the protagonists are soloists expressing how love is a big, dangerous country you just can't drive your legend through. They are expressing their devotion and admiration for each other but from afar. From the safe distance of history where neither one can be hurt, yet. In one short poem, billy says, "don't come/around here/there's death/around here/power/and fear/don't come/around here." In a lovely declaration, frida says:

"my bedroom is a bullring
the circle of my creation
the cycle of my battle
with the animal
the mirror

my canvas is my cape
my brush is my sword
I do metaphysical battle
With my body

Sweet torero of improvisation

My spontaneous movements
Stain the sand

I am showered with roses
My hair sweeping down
Into my face

I am naked in this bullring
And everyone is watching

It is frida's vulnerable declaration of self-knowledge and the burdens of fame that make it so vivid. Meanwhile, billy has his own problems: "they call me killer/but nothing is more violent/than love/nothing more intimate/than that possession." She is *aware* of the endgame and her body's role in that betrayal. Billy struggles for his identity in the universe, to become something less pestilential than just a poster boy for "ecstatic violence". Finally, frida states to billy and the world: "I'll make my exit pure . . he's just a flash/she's just an image/a spirit sign/take what you can find." This is as close as Frida Kahlo (and Tony Moffeit) will get to a benediction for two legendary figures who weren't lovers but shared a notoriety, a vulnerability and certainly the same death wish the universe usually reserves for those who die young.

For many years now Tony Moffeit's writing has sung the land, lore and mysticism of the southwest, his words have conjured black snake New Orleans. If the literary term "outlaw" means nothing else, it should lead us to believe that beyond academia, beyond institutions, out there on the streets of America, there has always been an impulse to creatively wail out loud, with the voice and words as instruments that has helped poetry gain an acceptance and accessibility it

LOS NIETOS PRESS
Helping local writers share their words

Hồng-Mỹ Basrai   liz gonzález   C.D. Courter

Linda Singer   Clifton Snider

LosNietosPress.com   LosNietosPress@gmail.com

Thanks Frank for all you do!

never had before, especially in the age of the internet. Many younger poets across America (and beyond) have embraced literary outlaw, if not in name, then in style and substance because of its easily recognizable sense of rebelliousness, defiance of traditional grammatical considerations, its colloquial energy. Its traditions embrace the Beats, surrealism, dada, the symbolists, the anarchy and individualism of the American West, noir films, jazz, blues and rock and roll.

Tony Moffeit's poetry has inhabited all of these at one time or another. You can feel their echoes in his words. Defiant, beautiful and immediate.

Sources:
Moffeit, Tony *billy the kid & frida kahlo* New Haven: Ye Old Font Shoppe, 2000.
Moffeit, Tony *Born to be Blue* San Pedro: LUMMOX Press, 2011
(Todd Moore) *Working the Wreckage of the American Poem: Todd Moore Remembered*
    edited by RD Armstrong, LUMMOX Press, 2011
Malpais Review Vol. 1, No. 1 summer 2010, edited by Gary Brower
Outlaw Poetry & Free Jazz Network (on line)

Mike Mahoney

33 Ways To "Make Common Words Uncommon Again"*

*Lawrence Ferlinghetti

1. Hold a noun down & tickle it until it reveals its other uses & shades.

2. Repeat a noun's name, or have the noun repeat its name aloud until it loses its own meaning to itself, then set it loose in your speech for the day.

3. Have your most commonly used words each blindfold themselves & spin in circles with their foreheads touching the top of a semicolon they're holding to the ground with one hand while trying not to spill a drop of their beer in the other, then have them chug their pint & tell 5 quick stories about their childhood, which you'll record & pick out the gems from (via mesh screen & a shuffling process you learned from your time in the backcountry) while you sort through with sharpened eraser & telescope.

4. Perform a shamanic act of medicine on them. Have the shaman drum and smoke as many cigarettes as he or she needs, for as long as they need to, until they can remove the malignant spirits inhabiting the inflicted word like elevator muzak.

5. Make a liquid of your common word. Grind it up like coffee beans or trim it to get the tea leaves & steep in hot water, or else alchemize through whatever means necessary to distill a tincture or potion. Either way, the idea is to make a beverage of your common word & drink it while urinating. The process of the word passing through your digestive system while your body is in a pleasant state of astonishment at this somewhat rare experience has a rejuvenating & medicinal effect on the word – sort of like going through a car wash, sweat lodge & psychedelic out-of-body experience simultaneously, all while sitting in a sauna.

6. Sometimes a simple jolt of the words' sense perceptions is enough – a tiny shock so it sees its same old letters afresh again. It's same old threads as sultan's silk & emperor's satin. If you think this may be all your word needs, give it paid time off to take a good long trip wherever it wants to go. The simple experience of returning home to itself after a long adventure away should do the trick.

7. Hold the word upside down over a very, very tall cliff, like Zen monks will hold initiates by the ankles. This vivid technique, if a little aggressive and, as a result, frowned upon by the standards of today, still undeniably holds a variety of deep & long-lasting psychological impacts for your participating word, not the least of which includes the shedding of its more common patterns & habits of appearance, of behavior & general engagement with other words, as, having just stared its own death in the face for a duration of time, will be so happy just to be alive & spoken, its entire world will seem a Heaven & everything in it an Angel.

8. "OK," you say to your common word, "OK, you think you're so smart? Think you know everything? Go ahead & try & measure the whole world by your one measly definition. And don't come back until you do!" Words can get cranky when they've been overused, exhausted, and this means sometimes you've got to be a strict parent or landlord. When the word returns, because it will, (they always will, they have no other place to go), it will be humbled. Defeated slightly. But this should already be giving way to a newly kindled openness & excitement to stretch itself, to put itself in more uncommon places, to experience more, simply put. It's gone out, seen a bit of the world, &

will likely sense a rejuvenating influence. If it doesn't, you can retire that word for a younger model. It's simply exhausted. It happens.

9. Have your word take a week or two, or more, for as long as it takes really, and track another word you both agree is bizarre & interesting. Unique in its habits & quite definitely uncommon, as far as words in these woods go. If nothing more, you & your word will bond a little more & get a few nights to camp out, to sleep under a shower of stars.

10. Wait until the word is asleep. Sneak in quietly & move his bed to another town entirely inside your head. He'll be forced to find new ways to fit in, new uses for himself to work & get along with all of his new neighbors.

11. Helicopter your word into a remove valley of wilderness in the dictionary you keep at your desk & tell him he has to find his own way back within 33 days or you'll write the word Wolf on 1,000 scraps & bits of paper & sprinkle them in. You don't need to worry about that word being common anymore – whether it makes it out or not.

12. Read Terence Mckenna's book True Hallucinations. Perform the same experiment with your word the brothers McKenna did on themselves at la Chorrera. You & your word are sure to never say another common thing ever again.

13. Step One: Bring your word to a boil in a large pot of Poetry. Turn to low heat & cover. In another pan, brown the meat of ancient wisdom, season with astrology, bits of archaeology & shredded dream. Add into the larger pot & stir. • Step Two: Turn the heat up. Add in 1 can each of love & heartbreak. Stir. Turn heat to low & let simmer 33 minutes. • Step Three: Add 3 paragraphs of your choice from either Marcel Proust, Francois-Rene de Chateaubriand, or Rene Crevel, and a book of Old-World maps. • Step Four: Last but never least, of course, add 3 oz of your favorite high-potency cannabis, finely ground up & decarbonized.

Also, you might consider here a few pinches to a healthy dollop of psilocybin.

14. Have your word fast & go on a Vision Quest in the remote pages of a thesaurus. Depending on the word & its history, be aware of the force you may have created.

15. Talk to the right people to obtain a pass & visiting time. Take your word to the closest major airport bookstore. Let them walk around & talk to the prisoners there…see where common words can end up…what a common life for a word can lead to. This should scare them straight.

16. Spend as many nights in areas known for sightings as it takes until you spot a UFO. Until a UFO spots you. Quickly, put the word (which is dressed in your clothing) in your place & hide. Stay hidden until you see it soar off with your word, becoming just another sequin in the fabric of night. Expect an uncommon signal from your word soon on its new life & meaning.

17. "Forget" your word in the car with the engine running & the setting appropriately set for the inappropriate act. Rush back in at the last moment & save your word. The NDE your word will have just had should trigger a lasting behavioral change. Or, if not, and your word doesn't have an ecstatic & life-changing, out-of-body near-death afterlife-glimpse experience, but only discovers you almost accidentally killed it on purpose, well, that will still result in a change from its common behavior won't it? Win—win.

18. Hold your word up to a source of light. The sun will do. Take note how little of the light is visible through your word. Hike to a nearby river & wash your word there, copiously, singing your family line's power songs softly to each of its letters. Wash each side well, & between each syllable. Now hold it back up to that same light. The same sun if you can manage. Take note how your previous rock-eclipse is now a rainbow-throwing prism.

19. When the sun rises make sure you're already out & waiting. Before the sun loses touch with the horizon & takes flight into sky, scan the horizon for anything unusual. It could be a glint of philosophy or the origins of a school of jellies, a heatwave shaped like a romantic crush – you'll know it when you see it. Spend the rest of the day hiking there & make camp when you arrive. The next morning at sunrise again, you'll bury your word in the earth up to its neck, so only its suffix sticks out. The goal here is a focused, revolving acupuncture by sun, moon & starlight, touching only the pineal & power points of the word's crown. Welcome it back into the tribe of your vocabulary with open arms after four days: three for magic to enter & do its thing, and the fourth to close everything back up.

20. Maybe your word just needs the surface things, the simple things in life. Try your word out in a new wardrobe of fonts, in different styles & colors, different sizes. See if it might like to be typewritten or embossed, letter-pressed or stenciled for a change. Debossed, stitched, emboldened or embroidered. Woodcut or calligraphied. Self-image is everything, even for words. (Maybe especially for words.)

21. If, as Tom Robbins says, there are no such things as synonyms, (& i believe he's correct), think of how often you're making your word look bad by using it so impulsively, so inconsiderately, ignorantly & without any thought, when what you mean in nearly every circumstance is something slightly different. With that in mind, draw a thick black line under your word, and encourage it to pick a few of its closer friends (you'll cover the bill) each day to go to work with it. Each time your word comes up it'll stick out as underlined, and its friends can jump in where appropriate, doing all the jobs your word has been filling in for for god knows how long. Imagine it like a kind of Mad-Libs. Just think how much it will get done

after your word is rested & recovered, when it has all its time back, all its energy back around for itself again.

22. Have your word take a vow of silence for a while, for an extended period, though continuing still to live with you – not dropping out of the world entirely, just not speaking as it normally would. The heightened awareness & laser-like clarity of all the realizations it discovers during this time, of all the revelations it has while in this nurturing cocoon of silence, will only deepen its being, expand & add to its impact on life & language when it returns, if it does return. Not all words decide to speak again.

23. Bury your word in a special place under the ancient doorway of two tall pines. Leave it there at least four days, but up to three months. Words have attractive & repellent qualities, electrical & metaphysical properties. This will ground all excess image, debris, poison & meaning, any pollution, any interference, any live wires & bad frequencies, spooky juju or funky vibes.

24. Fill the word with water. Purified is preferred, but not necessary. Once the word is filled up, stretch the opening out and get inside with your canoe. Row until you come upon an island with a single tower. (If there's more than a single tower you're too late – if there's more than a single tower & they're each belching smoke or any other kind of waste product, you're too late & it's too late to run – you'll have to bring the whole island down & won't be able to save yourself.) Beach your canoe. If there's only one tower, and no signs of advanced technology, the word's inner island is most likely still inhabited by a single tribe of images. But act fast, the very fact you're here means it won't last long, means there's something horribly wrong. Missionaries from every church, cause & corporation in the world below will soon descend on this helpless paradise of a word & battle to the death for control & power,

stake & claim. Your only job is to greet the native images there, share the goods given to you by their shaman in a dream you should have received by now, and spread the contents of the medicine bag he gave you in the same dream. The fine white grains will look like ripped bits, corners, sections & fistfuls of the entire world's cobwebs. They'll gleam with iridescence. You should feel like you can taste the most subtle amounts of lavender, of turquoise, night & indigo in the air – kind of a bruise colored earth smell. That's it. Like some New Testament parable with magic built in, there should be enough there in that small pouch to cover the entire island. Get the locals to help you spread it. Inside of an hour, an hour at most, an immense power will be felt as a membrane. A forcefield of intelligence growing up from & surrounding the island and expanding out. Invisible, tactful in its felt presence, yet felt by yourself & by the natives to be alive, living & aware, to have its own sentience, its own power & self-awareness. You can remain here if you wish – little to no time will pass below in your own world. But when you're ready, simply place your attention on the energyfield and your attention on returning. It will happen as so. You'll probably receive another dream in the coming days. Another visit from the word's inner shaman, smiling, probably holding out a small handful of mushrooms (now reported growing on the island for the first time) as a gift of thanks.

25. As with your own phone, how you can assign a certain song for an alarm or to a specific person calling, try and bell & collar your word with a super funky ass song it likes. This way, anytime it's brought near your vocal chords it will start dancing like a bear & won't come out so stiff & rigid in its common shape.

26. Go the political route & hire a few other words who don't know each other to dig up a little dirt. Place said dirt in a white envelope, or a larger yellow envelope if the dirt includes

NEW COLLECTION OF SPANISH POEMS
FROM LUMMOX PRESS -- $12
$12 AVAILABLE ON AMAZON BOOKS

dirty photographs. Slide the envelop across the table toward your word at lunch. Make it clear he's being blackmailed for better, more creative performance. Be clear without stating it outright. Your word may be doubling up & wearing a wire.

27. Go the kindergarten route & tattle-tell like a toddler to the Logos that so-&-so isn't doing its job, so-&-so isn't working or being original at all but rather giving every mouth a ride & whoring itself out to every common situation & comment around.

28. Read to your word. Read & read widely. Give your word lots of other words & images to play with & talk to, learn from & fight with. Creativity is a messy, poetic & evolving cauldron of process transforming according to the rule of metaphor, the momentum of a certain style, and the flexible law of novelty. An expansive vocabulary strengthens each word of it & sharpens the whole picture.

29. Scientifically, humans are discovering the benefits of microdosing psychedelics. This may work on words as well. Write the word Psilocybin on a small piece of paper & cut it up into very small bits, so that each letter may be made up of maybe 20-33 bits. Have your word consume 2-3 bits each day for 3 days, taking the 4th day off, then 2 days on, 1 day off. Continue each week. By the time your word is even halfway through the psilocybin you should already be noticing uncommon results.

30. Put your word under anesthesia. Roll it into the operating room. With great care & tremendous delicacy, replace its main organs with large crystals discovered in old mountain springs. Replace its heart with a fist-sized, crystal singing bowl. Sew up the incisions. Bless three handfuls of dirt & spit on them. Rub the mixture with love into the future scars to prevent infection & complete the chain of correspondences now activated by breath.

31. First boil a pot of water and have your word lean its suffix over with a towel over its head, breathing in the steam. This will loosen everything up. Next have the word stand on its head & say its name backwards 999 times. This should reverse whatever curse of overuse & shallow meaning has been cast upon it, whether intentionally or not, and set the toxic contents dripping out its top. Have some spare towels, a mop & bucket at the ready.

32. Adjust the letters of your word one by one – stretching them, giving them a short massage – then proceed with some good chiropractic work. Words are like living woodwinds: they can get out of tune, out of alignment with themselves from heavy use. As openings in their letters shift even a little out of place, the breath flowing through changes its motion, its pitch, how its circulating through the word. Stagnant spots appear. Like knots in our backs or shoulders. The word starts slouching, appearing & sounding always with the same stance, the same common posture. A quick work over should realign the words skeleton, its sonic structure, & work out any phonetic kinks.

33. Reconnect your word with its entire etymological tree. Let it get back in touch with its roots, its origins, its phonetic essence. Its original context & subsequent karmic layers, branches & tributaries of context, spelling, essence & meaning. Let your word rekindle the embers of its history within itself, all the odd bits & weird ends which weave its strange heritage. Its uncommon composition. Its bite, bark, warp & woof.

A DIVISON OF LUMMOX PRODUCTIONS

MOON IN THE BUCKET FUND

Promoting Poetry through Grants and scholarships

562 331-4351   poetraindog@gmail.com

Michael M. Meloan
MR. JEETER

ROBERT MASHED the gas pedal and held it down. The Fairlane sat back on its soft springs and made a loud whooshing sound. In a few seconds he was up to fifty-five, then he took it up to seventy.

"Slow down you idiot! Do you want to get busted?" said Petra. "Look…you are getting busted."

A cop going the other direction had seen us shoot past. The black-and-white whipped a screeching U-turn and kicked down into low. The Christmas tree came on as the sickening low-frequency drone of a 454 cubic inch Chrysler surged up from behind. Robert looked dazed by the flashing red and blue lights reflected in the rear view mirror. He took his foot off the accelerator and started to brake… then suddenly punched it again.

"NO! You JERK!" said Petra. She frantically rifled around in her purse, then threw a handful of joints out the window. Robert made a screaming hard right turn down a side street as a hubcap popped off and veered away from the car. The Fairlane raced down to the end of a small residential block. Julie was digging her fingernails into Robert's arm. My feet were locked against the dashboard.

Petra started screaming, "You fucking idiot asshole!"

Mr. Jeeter looked scared for once.

I can't let this happen," said Robert through clenched teeth.

Just as the cop came around the corner, Robert made another hard right. The rear end broke loose in mossy gutter water. He powered into the fishtail, and the car started swinging wildly from side-to-side. Robert frantically jerked the steering wheel back-and-forth fighting for control. His elbow nearly hit Julie in the face as he worked it. The tires were smoking,

but he stayed on the gas. The rear end was almost sideways when the right front wheel slammed into the curb with a bone jarring crash. The impact threw me against the door and jerked my neck as the Fairlane jumped the curb. It came to a stop with its hood right underneath a kitchen window. Robert was breathing fast. He threw it into reverse, backing off the lawn. Then he tried to drive down the street. Clattering grinding metal sounds came from beneath the car. As he floored it again, the tires spun hopelessly. A cloud of bluish rubber smoke enveloped us. The police cruiser pulled up and screeched to a halt. Intense white spotlights poured through the interior.

"Everybody—slowly get out of the car with your hands on your heads," said a voice over a bullhorn.

"It looks like an old coon, and a bunch of high school kids," said the cop to his partner, with the bullhorn still on.

"No backup, but I'll need a tow truck," said the second cop into the radio.

I stepped out with my hands on my head, and looked at the front wheel on my side. It was sticking sideways out of the wheel-well, with thick metal rods hanging loose.

"You tore the wheel off," I said to Robert.

"Shut up," said a big burly cop. "No talking unless I ask a question."

"Officer, I gotta tell you something. We don't even know these guys, we were just hitchhiking," said Julie.

"Fucking bitches," said Robert.

"Look, I told you all to shut up, and I mean it. Now!" said the cop, as he removed an empty bottle of Colt 45 from the back seat. "Open the trunk," he said to Robert.

Robert walked around to the back and popped open the trunk. The cop took out the cardboard box with the last full bottle of 45 in it. He reached in again and threw a plaid blanket onto the ground, then a small wicker picnic basket. Something broke inside the basket.

"Hey, be careful with that stuff!" yelled Robert.

"Shut the fuck up," said the cop.

"Fuck you," said Robert under his breath.

"What did you say, you little piece-of-shit?" said the cop, walking toward him.

"Nothing," said Robert softly.

People had started coming out of their houses on both sides of the street. They stood on their lawns and stared as red and blue lights raced across their faces. Robert breathed unevenly as he watched the burly cop throw his mother's coat onto the ground. Robert's eyes were riveted on the inside of the trunk as the other cop took out a legal folder and tossed it onto the sidewalk. It opened up, and the typed documents started blowing away. Robert leaped forward and grabbed the handles of his mother's bowling ball, yanking it from the trunk. Twisting his body back-and-forth, he swung the ball wildly trying to hit the smaller cop in the stomach.

"FUCKING ASSHOLES! Leave my mother's shit alone!" he screamed. The big cop grabbed him and jerked the bowling ball out of his hands, fiercely twisting Robert's arm behind his back.

"Oh shiiit!" Robert screamed.

Julie and Petra took off like a shot, running across the street. They were fast.

"Go after 'em Frank!" yelled the cop to his partner. Frank turned and ran. The big cop snapped thick chrome handcuffs around Robert's wrists. Mr. Jeeter and I looked at each other.

"Le's get on out o' here," he whispered. "Follow me."

As the cop pushed Robert's head down into the back seat of the squad car, Mr. Jeeter and I backed away from the scene. Another squad car turned the corner at the end of the block. We ducked around the side of a house and into the alley.

"They're getting away!" yelled one of the neighbors.

"We've got to run. Can you run?" I asked Mr. Jeeter.

"I can run some," he said.

We took off down the alley and through a side yard with no fence. Mr. Jeeter was breathing hard, but he could run. A cop was cruising down the street as we came out from behind some bushes. We jumped back into the darkness and got down on the grass between the houses. The police were shining lights everywhere as they drove by. It was a manhunt.

Dogs barked all over the neighborhood as we cut through more side streets and made our way to the Century Drive-In Theater. It was nearly deserted inside, so we sat down on the still-warm asphalt and watched a movie where Paul Newman was eating one hard boiled egg after another until his stomach bulged out like a watermelon. I pulled a metal speaker off a pole and turned up the sound. A couple of squad cars cruised past out on Century Boulevard, but they couldn't see us.

After about 20 minutes, Mr. Jeeter and I started up the hill toward Crenshaw Boulevard. There was a small 24 hour burger stand with a huge neon Indian head on top. It had glowing white teeth, and its eye winked over-and-over. Two words flashed underneath, AH-HA, AH-HA. A red neon feather towered about ten feet above the head.

"Let's go to that place for a burger and some coffee," said Mr. Jeeter.

"Aren't places like that big cop hangouts?" I asked.

"I think they still busy cruising 'round the houses," he said. "Besides, it won' take long."

We went to the takeout window and ordered two cheeseburgers, an order of fries, and two large cups of coffee. Long white florescent tubes lined the ceiling—it was painfully bright. The old woman at the order window was staring at us, like she knew we were on the run. We sat at the wooden picnic tables around the side, away from the street. When the food came, we took the cups and the bag around back into the alley and sat on a concrete ledge next to a stinky trash dumpster under a streetlight. The burgers were covered with thin greasy cheese; the coffee was hot and strong. I'd never tried coffee before.

"This was quite a night, youngblood," said Mr. Jeeter, as he looked up at me while taking a drink. "But I think it's time for you and me to split up. We look a kinda strange together," he laughed.

As we both took big drinks of coffee, I felt like I was seeing him for the first time. I noticed his square jaw, black and gray stubble beard, flat nose, and dark piercing eyes. He looked cool. It seemed like a long time ago that we had first met at the liquor store. There was a long pause.

"I was afraid to have sex with those girls," I said finally.

"I was too," he said. "Not jus' because I was wonderin' if I could get it up. I think they had the Voudou. Maybe tha's why we crashed."

"What do you mean, *the Voudou*?"

"That wild little thing..her eyes look funny. You didn' see nothin' strange about the way she look?"

"She looked…a little crazy," I said.

"Tha's it, but even mo'. You know, they's women down in N'Orleans, they cast some spells. When she get a little older, I think maybe she could be one of them. Has to do with the female powers. You remember how she jus' appear out of nowhere? Tha's how they do. They come up on you when yo' mind is in a certain way. Sometimes they give a message, and sometime they jus' want to mess with yo' head. It's never when you expect it, but you gotta roll with it when it come. Your friend's the one thas' got a whammy on him."

"You mean a curse?"

"Right," said Mr. Jeeter. "But he still got a chance. They didn' have time to work out the full mojo."

"Why didn't you tell us that before?" I asked.

"I didn't know before. It come on me about the time that little thing move in to kiss me," he said. "She looked in my eyes…and man, it was somethin' else. I've seen that look befo'."

Mr. Jeeter reached over and put the last two cigarettes in my shirt pocket, then wadded up the pack. "I wouldn' worry, the biggest whammy he got to deal with right now is what his mamma gonna do when she find out he tore the wheel off her brand new ride."

We both started laughing, then Mr. Jeeter started coughing.

"I gotta get on back," he said. "Too much excitement fo' one night."

He put his hand on my shoulder and steadied himself as he stood up. Then we shook. His hand was dry and leathery. He paused and locked onto my eyes for a long moment, smiling a little. Then he turned and started walking toward the street.

"Take care of yourself youngblood," he said, without looking back. "Don't forget to make them rhymes."

I tried to say something as I watched him walk down the alley, but I couldn't. The AH-HA Indian was winking with that white neon eyelid.

The neighborhood was dark, except for the gigantic time and temperature tower on top of the California Federal bank building—2:31 AM, in thousands of tiny light bulbs. It was warm and crystal clear—the Santa Anas were really blowing. I headed east on Century Boulevard at the far end of the junior high. More dogs barked as I cut through a side yard and walked along a residential street. My parents were going to be furious, but I didn't care. I'd deal with that when I got there. A tumbleweed rolled down the blacktop. I could feel the hot wind.

Goodbye Mr. Jeeter.

Charles Plymell
EATING AND DRINKING WITH THE BEATS (PART TWO)
CONTINUED FROM LUMMOX 8 (2019)

PAM, ELIZABETH and I went on vacation to the city. Burroughs graciously gave us his loft below Centre St. in the financial district while he and James went abroad. There was a grand (old) piano. Patty Smith called him daily on his answering machine. Upon their return, James fixed us a light dinner and Bill downed a few glasses of Vodka.

Through Elliott Coleman at Hopkins, we got Allen the F. Scott Fitzgerald room across from the Homewood Campus for a few days. We had moved back to Baltimore. We had Allen for dinner at our place there for a few meals and then helped him find a room at the Albion Hotel, where he studied Blake for a week or so. Near the Albion Hotel was a coffee shop that served a Baltimore oddity: A hot dog rolled up in a slice of baloney and slice of Velveeta cheese all hot and greasy on a bun. I mentioned it years later, thinking I imagined it, to Roxie Powell, who worked at the Mayor's office nearby. He said he loved them and ate them all the time. We fared better during crab season when Robert Bly visited us. I was teaching at St. Mary's College in Maryland, and we had fresh crab catch.

After my book signing party at the Gotham for Trashing of America, the Hornicks took Pam, me, Mary, Claude, Jean-Louis Brau to a very expensive Italian restaurant where I had "Hay and Straw" at about a hundred dollars a plate. Jean-Louis was talking about his "Situationist Party" in France. Our hosts seemed shocked to be in the presence of real revolutionaries. We got stinking drunk and in the restroom Claude and Jean-Louis started spewing ethnic slurs. I repeated them at the table, which included Allen. Lita Hornick said she had never witness such behavior "since Leroy Jones". She never spoke to me again.

We had moved to another house in Cherry Valley by the time Allen brought his stepmother to lunch with us at the notorious "Bowling Alley" in Cherry Valley where the waitresses slung burnt toast and would say, amicably, that if we didn't like it, to fix it ourselves. As on many occasions, Allen stopped at our house for soup or whatever Pam was fixing. Allen knew good soup and knew Pam's cooking, but one time his veggie driver embarrassed him by declining because it was made with chicken broth. Pam brought the driver a plate of veggie compost.

Burroughs assigned to Huncke the gift of ferreting. In one of Huncke's visits to us in Baltimore, we took him to the train station. He was ever so polite and tight and had given an incredible reading with me and Bremser at an all-night dopester bar. He spotted a fancy diner and said it looked "Right." We all ordered hamburgers, french fries and coffee. The coffee and fries were all right. The hamburger was more than right. Just the right amount of leftover grease slightly grilled on generous buns. The hamburger had been hand pattied, cooked to order. Thin slices of onion, tomatoes, pickles with the lettuce to the side unwilted. We were high of course, and ate the American icon with relish.

James Grauerholz had invited me to read in Lawrence. My son, Billy and I were visiting Kansas, my home state and on to Wichita from Lawrence. Rob Melton at K.U. had scored us a place to stay on campus. I had my mother's pump 22 rifle with us that she had used to feed us kids jackrabbits (Hoover Steaks) during the Great Depression. James fixed us a good sirloin and said to bring the rifle over, that Bill would want to see it. Bill balanced it on one finger remarking how good it was made saying, "They don't make 'em like this anymore. Feel it Charley, just like a woman's leg!" He aimed it around the house and pumped it and pulled the trigger. He then got out his loaded 38 Special and slapped it in my hand. "Feel this," he said, "It'll stop anyone in their tracks." He got out his collection of knives to show Billy and me, having a story for each one. We looked over the knifes some more while James fixed dinner. Bill rolled a joint and passed it to me. I had an article I was reading about the hallucinogenic properties under a frog's skin that had been found in Australia. Bill made up a story of kids going out and skinning the frogs and sucking out the chemicals. James served us one of his wonderfully simple meals of vegetables and steak. Bill drank and smoked poking around at his excellent plate as a kid would, not eating much. After we had finished, James brought out a big bowl of gum drops. Bill grabbed a handful and crammed them in his mouth with some falling into his plate. It was night and Bill heard a noise out back. He had been feeding a critter and determined it was a raccoon by its eating habits. He got a flashlight and took Billy out to search for it. Later James said that it was a memorable evening and it was certainly a great evening for an eight-year old.

Another time, Pam, Billy and I stopped for James' dinner at the Burroughs' cottage. James fixed steak, a favorite of Pam's. "How old's the boy?" He asked Pam, in a typical Midwestern idiom. Billy was eleven then. Bill rolled a joint

and poured the Vodka. He was just getting into painting. He brought out some paintings and told us to select one each. He said "this is great art, Charley. Look at them, different things happen in them." Unfortunately, I had to sell them later to pay for the trip. He then got out his blow dart gun, put a dart in it and put it to his mouth. I told Billy to stand in back of us. Bill aim it at the front door and blew the dart in it. "Lucky someone wasn't coming in", Billy said. Bill tried to get it out of the door but couldn't budge it. He got a pair of pliers and pulled it out. I was coming back from Ulysses, Kansas, out on the plains, where I grew up. But I did bring the paintings back to Cherry Valley and put them outside and different shapes did form in them. He then brought out a montage he had made and sat me and Billy down to watch as he, like an old carny, moved about to change shapes. Pam mentioned she would like to do another small book and have S. Clay Wilson illustrate it. She had done Cobblestone Gardens, one which I sent Bill a bunch of old photos to select from for the text. He rummaged around in his bedroom and got a bunch of typed pages. "Here's some I'm working on. Let me know if you need more." He said S. Clay would be a good choice for the illustrations. We called it *Tornado Alley.*

It was in November 1996, Ralph Ackerman and I arrived by train, after spending until daybreak while the railcars humped around in Kansas City. Lawrence pre-dawn. Crossing the East/West border at the Missouri River. Ralph was taking me to San Francisco for an event, the trip a part of it. We got a motel. Pat O'Connor and Rayl met on Mass Ave in Lawrence. Just like the old days when we arrived on time, whenever that was, with all our equipment, whatever that was. Burroughs had his show up. After the auditorium was the reception. It was packed with high culture. Ginsberg and Burroughs were signing autographs. They got a chair for me in the middle, and I started signing with them. There so many lines it was as if the signing was the event, and it didn't matter who I was, I was sitting between them, so my signature must be worth something. James fixed us lamb chops that evening at Burroughs' cottage. Allen helped James with the dishes. Bill and I sat at the table. He was not smoking his English cigarettes, so I could not bum. He put the catalog for his show on the table. "Look at that, Charley" he would say. "A beautiful production, don't you think?" He showed me the paintings in it, explaining each one. He was quite proud of the book and said it was reasonably priced at $25. I asked him for that one, just to put him on a bit. I'll never forget the look of polite embarrassment, wanting to be generous but won't be conned look. He smiled pleasantly, and said, "not this one." He summoned me to his bedroom and Allen made some comments about his chambers, putting some magic to the evening. Bill took out his stash from his drawer with the 38. He told me to sit at his dresser and roll a joint. Allen went to the supermarket with James to get Allen special foods. Ralph wasn't eating. He had throat cancer. "Dr." Burroughs engaged him in medical talk about his condition. Bill, Allen and I each had undergone heart problems in the recent past. The evening had a ceremonial, soiree ambiance. Bill wasn't drinking or smoking. After dinner, James wrote a poem and was encouraged to read it. Afterwards, he handed it to Allen, who began editing it. James was complimentary for having the honor. Allen, who was a professor at City College said humbly, "That's my job." The conversation turned, at my direction to the questions for the panel raised by members of the audience at the lecture, earlier. Those members on the panel were asked what their all-time favorite lines were. Bill quoted Tomorrow, tomorrow tomorrow, and Allen quoted the couplet from Shakespeare's sonnet "in black ink, my love may still shine bright." I mentioned that they both quoted Shakespeare and Allen wasn't sure

of the lines. I recited the whole sonnet and told him it was easier to begin at the beginning with it. Allen was surprised I could recite the whole sonnet. Bill peevishly tried to interrupt me about midway through and James gently put his hand on his shoulder.

Ginsberg read my "heart attack" poem to Bill, James, and Ralph Ackerman, remarking about some lines reminding him of Shakespeare. Bill absorbed them, as he seemed to do with words: with larger language components, he seemed ready to cut them up and re-assemble them his mind, in cartridges ready to fire. Allen then made some minor editorial marks on the poem.

Bill went to his bedroom and put on his pyjamas and prowled deliberately around the house, feeling his canes. He picked up his Mexican-carved sugar skull and talk about it, handing it around. During dinner, Allen talked ostensibly about health and particularly about his diet. He could not eat sugar. I said to Bill, "Well at least Allen won't eat your skull." Bill chuckled and answered. "No, Ginsberg won't eat my skull."

James and I went outside the house to look at the Kansas sky and admire the big cottonwood tree in the yard. Bill came out on the porch clearly restless as in minutes to go. He had been "out there" so he seemed to like being at home with friends, prowling, like one of his cats. His living space always had awesome feeling. That was the last time Allen saw Bill.

S. Clay Wilson eats everything. I think it is because he cannot drive. Nor swim. Robert Williams told me that if S. Clay was in a car by himself in a flood, he'd really be up shit creek. In San Francisco, Wilson took Glenn Todd and me to a Mexican Restaurant in the Mission district, S.F. He knew I liked Chili Rellenos and told me this was the spot. He insisted on the Peach Daiquiris. Just right. Later, and it was a long day and night, we went to a Chinese Restaurant on Polk St. S, Clay ate all our left-overs and sucked Glenn's duck bones clean. Next day, he took us to his friend Susan's house in Berkeley. She fixed an exquisite meal of chicken breasts and rice, and a fresh vinaigrette of fresh leaves from her garden. It was like Malanga's salad.

Easter 1997 we met S. Clay in N.Y.C., got blasted and planned to visit Allen. About 11:00 we decided it was too late in the evening to call: we didn't know it at the time, but Allen lay dying. We came to Cherry Valley for a few days. Wilson bought me an Easter chocolate wrench at Dean and Deluca's. Pam got all the sandwich makings and we scored some Elephant beer. Pam fixed a great meal for S. Clay, but he had run down to the Quickway and ordered a large sub. He ate that for an appetizer and then finished his meal, then grabbed Pam's father's sword and played pirate. We drank, smoked and ate for the next few days, bringing the rest of the food from D&D's to Claude and Mary, who lived about an hour away.

In the spring of '97, I drove from Cherry Valley to Missoula, Montana to pick up my son after his freshman year at the University of Montana. On the way back, we stayed with Patricia Elliott, a grand gatherer of fine people. Her family was in the wrecking and salvage business in Lawrence, and she provided Bill with the right doors to shoot. She called Bill as we were leaving and he said to come on by. He had been chatting with one of his friends, a sculptor, a soldier of fortune-looking guy also into guns and knives, etc. who had some mutilated hand guns with him, ones that had been run over by tanks in an urban gun program of some sort. He was going to weld one to his metal sculpture and wanted Bill to shoot some high ballistics through it the next day. He handed the guns around. Bill looked at it, and slightly indignant, aware of the old teachings of his class...to take care of things...said, "I don't know why they'd want to do this to a perfectly nice Colt."

After his friend left, he talked to Billy about college. Billy told him that he was dropping out for a while. He didn't want to have the debt. Bill totally ridiculed the astronomical costs for college. And for what? He had a litany of what was taught and who taught the courses. He agreed with Billy that the costs were too high for average young white males. Bill looked melancholy out the window toward Montana, long ago. "My father used to take me fly fishing in Missoula" he said. Later I told Billy he should have asked him some questions. I asked Bill to sign a copy of *Western Lands* for Billy. Pointing to me he said "... An I have something for you, too." "Oh," I said. "What does it look like. Maybe I can help you find it." It comes in a bottle. He searched around the living room and his bedroom. I followed him around. He seemed remarkably nice; having lost my stash, I would have been aggravated. He said it was a bottle of Codeine. He had signed a book to me "Codeine Charley, all the best Rx." He couldn't find the bottle, so he took me to his medicine cabinet. "Can you take Methadone?" he asked. I said "Yes." He had two small capsules. "I don't know what your system can take, but drink what you want." I told him that Huncke had once sent me some in an old perfume bottle, complete with Dr. Huncke's instructions and warnings. I finished the one and downed most of the other capsule. I told him maybe I should finish it off, that I had a bug I caught in Missoula. He said he wasn't worried about drinking after me. I left a small amount in the cap.

I told him we should push on to St Louie before getting a motel that night. He said. "That will kick in about the other side of Kansas City. Billy got behind the wheel as we waved goodbye. "Via con Dios," Bill waved with his arm making a generous curve over his head. "What a great old man," we said. I crawled in the back of the car and went to sleep. "A Johnson to the last" I thought as I drifted off.

Linda Singer
A MASKED WOMAN TAKES A WALK

I'VE WALKED to the Rivera Village just blocks from home. The face mask is making my nose run and cheeks sweat. I hate it. I can't breathe. When I breathe, my sunglasses fog up. My nose itches, my mouth inches, my eyes itch. I've come to deposit a check. I stare at the bank's ATM machine. How can I use it safely? I get a Kleenex out and use it to place my debit card in the slot, use it the punch in my password code, but when the screen comes up, it needs heat to respond to commands. I use the backside of my hand to indicate that I want to deposit a check, I use the backside of my hand to confirm the amount. I retrieve the card and toss the Kleenex when finished.

"This is bullshit!" I say to the heavens.

A reply comes, "Who you talking to?"

"Is this how you run things?" I ask. "Piss poor, if you ask me."

"Nobody asked you," the heavens answer.

"Why do you sound like Groucho Marks?" I ask.

"That's your projection," the voice has changed to Betty Davis.

"Hey, I like it when she uses my voice," I hear Groucho say in the background. "I get bored up here kid. Too much singing and preaching. Go ahead, Linda. you have my permission. Use my voice."

I sit down on a bench in front of my Wells Fargo, next to my closed Starbucks. I notice a couple of homeless men wrapped in blankets on an opposite bench staring at me. One has dark hair and a messy beard. The second one is white headed and pink faced. They seem interested in the conversation I'm having.

"My god sounds like Merv Griffin," the dark-haired guy says. "I miss Merv."

Okay, so now, I'm having a three-way conversation with god and a couple of street people sitting on a bench. I reach into my purse to get something to wipe my nose and notice that the two homeless guys are looking at me with concerned stares. They're worried about me infecting them .

"It's only "old lady leaky nose"," I say. "I've had it for years."

They relax back on to their bench. "Could you give me some change. I'd like something to warm me up," the older one asks.

"Tell you what," I say, "I'll go across the street to Coffee, Tea or Me and get you whatever you want."

"My kinda girl," Betty Davis says.

I take their orders for breakfast biscuits and cappuccinos and cross the street to order a take out, the only thing being offered in the village these days.

When I return, the dark-haired guy says, "Merv says he forgives you for saying bullshit."

"Thanks," I say, "I was just venting anyway. If there is a god, I figure that he, she or it would understand and permit a little venting, don't you?"

Both men nod at me and take their food and drink. I decide to walk home and stop being such a whiner. I'm in a position to buy food for someone else and I have a place to go for shelter. I'm blessed. Thank you Merv.

GREETINGS FROM PITTSBURGH AND JUDY ROBINSON!!

William Smith

Rick Smith
SNOWED IN WITH CARL SANDBURG

IN 1956, we moved from a 2-bedroom apartment near 1st Avenue and 22nd Street in Manhattan to a converted barn in Pineville (population under 600). It was something about a more lenient tax structure for an artist in Pennsylvania. The barn was on two acres and only 65 miles from New York. My sister Kim was already 5; the two of us had been sharing our bedroom with an enormous etching press. The master bedroom doubled as dad's studio. It was time for a bigger place. I didn't want to move. I loved growing up in the city. I had lots of friends, loved the Yankees and rock and roll was coming in. I wasn't sure they had that in Pennsylvania. It turned out, fortunately, to be very much alive out there and, best of all, Kim and I had our own rooms. Mom and dad had a huge bedroom overlooking onion grass and a row of tulips marching out to the Windy Bush Road… our new address. Dad's studio space was enough for easels, frame racks, posters and the damn etching press. He was still within easy drive time of the art directors, costume rental warehouses, framers and photo studios he needed for his commissions from The Saturday Evening Post, Reader's Digest and the various book publishers who kept him working. Kim, Mom, neighbors and strangers could find themselves modeling for dad and then recognizing themselves in a national magazine or on a book cover. Mom might be Catherine The Great one month and a barfly the next. I could be Abe Lincoln as a young boy one month and Hamlet the next. Kim is the little girl drawing on the pavement on page 33 of Carl Sandburg's "Wind Song". That's her, too, arms around him on the back cover.

Those early April east coast storms: the

Editor's note: *Carl August Sandburg was an American poet, biographer, journalist, and editor. He won three Pulitzer Prizes: two for his poetry and one for his biography of Abraham Lincoln. During his lifetime, Sandburg was widely regarded as "a major figure in contemporary literature", especially for volumes of his collected verse, including Chicago Poems, Cornhuskers, and Smoke and Steel. He enjoyed "unrivaled appeal as a poet in his day, perhaps because the breadth of his experiences connected him with so many strands of American life", and at his death in 1967, President Lyndon B. Johnson observed that "Carl Sandburg was more than the voice of America, more than the poet of its strength and genius. He was America." And yet, as inconceivable as it is for me to believe, many Americans aren't familiar with his work.*

William Smith

sky begins to brood, clouds move in fast and a light flurry drifts down but it quickly becomes a dense sweeping deluge where visibility becomes nearly zero and silence envelopes the landscape. It's beautiful, really, unless you're on the roads. It'll snow steadily for two, three, maybe four days until, finally, one morning, the sky will be blue and the sunlight reflecting off all that white will nearly blind you. There is a translucence to everything after those storms. The power lines, heavy with ice, droop and look and like necklaces draped between the power poles. The tree branches look to be encased in Lucite, glassy and jewel like; they start dripping once the sun hits them. When these storm fronts came in, we'd lose power, the pipes would freeze and we'd boil snow for drinking water. The whole family would sleep on the floor in front of our river rock fireplace. We'd have to use the shovel just to clear the five foot drifts, to make a path to the firewood. We were stuck, sometimes for days. No school, roads closed and a one mile trek to the Pineville General Store and post office up on Route 413, where snowplows and generators kept things going.

For years, Sandburg had been visiting our New York City apartment whenever he was in town from his home in Flat Rock, North Carolina. My sister Kim took her first steps into his arms back in 1952. And when we moved to Pennsylvania, he'd visit and dad would often sketch him while they talked. Dad ended up doing a terrific pencil drawing of Sandburg's profile which appeared on the cover of "Harvest Poems" and also on an 8 cent U.S. postage stamp in the 1970's. Dad's photos and drawings graced the covers of several of Sandburg's books and record albums, but probably the best known of all dad's work that came out of that relationship was the large oil portrait that now hangs in the National Portrait Gallery in Washington, D.C. He was, I think, the only artist to paint Sandburg from life.

Sandburg was in Pineville sitting for that portrait in early spring, 1959 when one of those storms hit Bucks County so hard that we were snowed in for 4 days. During that week, I slept in front of the fireplace and Sandburg took my bedroom. He told me one morning that he liked the books in my collection and that he had fallen asleep reading "Greatest Moments In Baseball". He had to reach past William Blake, Joseph Campbell, Pearl Buck and Babe Pinelli to get to that book. Born in Illinois, he was a ferocious Chicago baseball fan; he probably got wrapped up in tales of Stan Hack or Dizzy Dean. A Yankee fan, he was not. Being from Illinois, he was used to weather like this and worse. He settled in for the long haul. He and dad were the yin and yang. Sandburg spoke slowly and seemed calm and relaxed, almost meditative, Dad was antsy and unnerved by the delay. He was impatient and did a lot of sighing and pacing.

I don't know how much painting was accomplished that week. The windows were tall in Dad's studio and they let in north light but the light didn't last long. It was amazing how Mom was able to feed the house during these storms. Before Sandburg's arrival, she put in a stock of his favored goat's milk and, during the storm, she was able to appropriate some cod from a neighbor. The fireplace was built for northeast winters… deep and wide for cooking and for cutting the chill of those freezing nights. Mom's family was 7th generation Parisienne; for Mom, cooking like a pioneer was a stretch, but she pulled it off. At night, after a candlelit dinner, Sandburg would pull out a guitar and sing. One of his many books was "The American Song Bag", an archival collection of folk songs from all sectors of our culture. He plowed through such classics as "C. C. Rider" and "Frankie and Johnny". He was a strummer really, but he knew the music and had a wonderful resonating tenor which also served him well at his book signings and poetry readings. A lot of the after dinner music and conversation was taped on dad's newfangled Tannhauser reel to reel deck. You can hear Sandburg singing and playing if you can find the studio recording, "Carl Sandburg Sings his American Song Bag," I've seen it online.

The conversations on the tapes were spirited, funny and intelligent. Sandburg and dad had really become friends and kindred spirits. They both agreed that Stevenson and not Eisenhower should have become the 34th president; they both recognized McCarthyism for the threat to privacy and freedom of expression that it was. Sandburg was actively supportive of the working class as he made clear in such works such as "Smoke and Steel" and "The People, Yes". He was also an astute observer of character, recognizing and documenting my dad's "galloping anxiety" in his poem, "Bill Smith". He was a poet for the every-man, a street poet more than an academic, and yet he firmly established his formidable scholarly skills in the exhaustive multi-volume biography of one of his heroes, Abraham Lincoln. He could work both sides of the literary street.

Sometimes, when you're a kid, you don't realize what's really going on until it's long over. I remember vividly my English teacher that year was Michael Casey. The day before the storm, I came into the studio after school waxing forth about newly learned poetry forms from Casey. Synedoche, a tactic of implication, was one of them. Sandburg seemed impressed. In History, I was writing a paper about the Lincoln presidency. I challenged Sandburg with the question, "Who, in Lincoln's Cabinet, didn't wear a beard?" He turned it around on me with, "Are you asking about beards or just whiskers?" Now, when it dawns on me that Carl Sandburg got snowed in with us, slept in my bed, talked baseball with me and led impromptu sing-alongs at our dinner table, I smile in wonder.

A Bucks County snow storm, frozen pumps, downed power lines, closed back roads and Sandburg's sweet tenor drifting across a candlelit room, still aglow in my memory of those long ago winter nights.

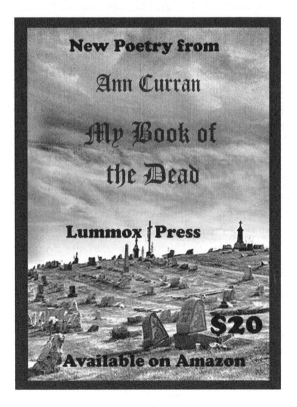

New Poetry from

Ann Curran

My Book of the Dead

Lummox Press

$20

Available on Amazon

BOOK REVIEW *by Nancy Shiffrin*

THE COLLECTED POEMS BY SYLVIA PLATH

HARPER & ROW 1981

"TO MY knowledge, she never scrapped any of her poetic efforts," writes Ted Hughes, in his introduction to Sylvia Plath's collected poems. "With one or two exceptions, she brought every piece she worked on to some final form acceptable to her, rejecting at most the odd verse, or a false head or a false tail. Her attitude to her verse was artisan-like: if she couldn't get a table out of the material, she was quite happy to get a chair, or even a toy. The end product for her was not so much a successful poem, as something that had temporarily exhausted her ingenuity."

The collection is essentially a chronological arrangement of those of Plath's poems written between 1956 and 1963. In addition, there is the introduction by Hughes, there are extensive notes, and an appendix of 50 poems written before 1956, (deceptively called juvenilia and worth reading for their intrinisic value as well as for information on the poet's development. There is a solitary attempt at translation: a poem by Rilke.

The manner of Plath's death is handled in the notes: "On 11 February (1963) she died by her own hand." Speculation about his most talked about literary suicide is clearly discouraged.

We may infer from the brevity of the introduction, and the austerity of the notes, a tacit request from husband and editor to concentrate on the artist's rich gifts. "Even her handwritten pages", Hughes writes are "as warm with startling, beautiful phrases... many of them in no way less remarkable than the ones she eventually picked out to make her poem".

There is evidence of her abundance in the lines she could afford to throw away, or at least leave in manuscript form and never finalize. Here are a few lines from "Stings", in which Hughes see "the first stirrings " of the celebrated "Bee" sequence. (Plath's father had been a bee-keeper; she kept bees herself),

> After, they stagger and weave, under no
> banner
> After, they crawl
> Dispatched, into the trenches of grass
> Ossifying like junked statues
> Gelded and wingless. Not heroes. Not
> heroes.

More jewels: these lines, part of the exploratory writing for the poem, "Fever 103".

> ... Here is the beauty
> of cool mouths and hands open and natu-
> ral as roses.
> My glass of water refract the morning.
> My baby is sleeping.

About the poem, Plath said, "it is about two kinds of fire – the fires of hell, which merely agonize, and the fires of heaven, which purify. During the poem, the first sort of fire suffers itself into the second." The closest lines in the published poem read;

> Am a pure acetylene
> Virgin
> Attended by roses...
> (My selves dissolving, old whore petti-
> coats)--
> To Paradise.

It is very difficult to honor the editor's wishes and refrain from speculation as to what Plath's life would have been like if she could have left herself some of the breath and lyricism of the earlier lines, if she had not such a compulsion to refine, if she had not been under such pressure, if she had not struggled to bring every tidbit of material to fruition, if she had not written three poems a day in the last year of her life; these in the early hours before her young children awakened, if there had been more forgiveness in her life.

I must confess that receipt of this book for review sent me scurrying to gather all of the books I own which mention Plath: *Women and Madness,* by Phyllis Chesler, which presents her as a martyr to the feminine mystique, *The Savage God,* by the Hughes's friend, Alvarez, who would have u s believe that the suicide was a mistake and Plath was to be rescued, *Sylvia Plath* by critic Caroline Barnard which says we can't separate life from work, then warns of hasty conclusions, most poignantly, Plath's own *Letters Home* edited by her mother Aurelia Schober Plath, when read in conjunction with this chronological arrangement of the poems, betrays the wrenching split between Plath's art and her life.

I was fascinated by Plath's own interpretation of her work as evidenced by her introductions to the BBC readings. About "Nick and the Candlestick" she wrote, "a mother nurses her baby son by candlelight and finds in him a beauty which, while it may not ward off the world's ill...does redeem her share of it". Still, it is a terrifying poem for a mother to write about her baby; the imagery of prehistoric caves, and lethal atoms belies the redemption she argues for at the end.

About "Lady Lazarus", one of her most quoted poems, she wrote, "The speaker is a woman who has the grit and terrible gift of being reborn. The only trouble is, she has to die first. She is the Phoenix, the libertarian spirit...She is also just a good, plain, very resourceful woman". The last line we must take as grim humor, a gallows humor reflected everywhere in the poems, particularly in this one where the "good, plain, resourceful woman", rises from her personal holocaust to "eat men like air". If only she had.

It is difficult to get away from the question: to what extent was Plath's death obsession, indeed, her death itself, necessary to her art and craft? I was initially distressed by the exclusion of the personal life from the introduction and notes to this volume. Did not Hughes, I asked myself, have any light to shed on the matter? Anything he was willing to say? Any personal emotion to express?

Increasingly, however, my attention was drawn to the surprises and discoveries in the work itself; the previously uncollected poems, most notably "Dialogue Over a Ouija Board", a verse dialogue included in the notes to "Ouija", the poem, "Queen Mary's Garden" which "she seems to have finished", Hughes writes, "but never included in her file". I found myself admiring the editorial labor involved in unearthing, dating and bringing together all this material.

I concluded, finally, that Hughes had made the correct choice of emphasis, that suicide is as much a mystery as art, that little enlightening has yet been said about the former, in spite of valiant attempts. That it is art, even when death-ridden, and craft that we can fruitfully discuss, that is of enduring value. In short, what Hughes has given us here is an awesome testimony from one fine artist to another.

STITCHES & SCARS

poems

Vachine
FIRST COLLECTION OF POETRY -- NEW
FROM LUMMOX PRESS -- $20.00
AVAILABLE ON AMAZON BOOKS

CONTRIBUTORS

Matt Amott is a poet, musician and photographer who rambles around the Pacific Northwest. He is co-founder and co-editor of Six Ft. Swell Press and has been published in numerous collections as well as three books of his own, *THE COAST IS CLEAR* (Six Ft. Swells Press), *GET WELL SOON* and *THE MEMORY OF HER* (both on Epic Rites Press). He can be reached and purchases made at Amazon and *www.sixftswellspress.com*

RD Armstrong aka Raindog has 18 chapbooks and 9 books to his name and has been published in over 300 poetry magazines, anthologies and e-zines. He's responsible for making all this happen; he also operates the LUMMOX Press which has published over 100 issues of the LUMMOX Journal; and nearly 150 other titles including the chapbook series Little Red Books and the Respect perfect bound collections. The LUMMOX Poetry Anthology is one of his most important projects. Since 2015, he has been relying, in part, on poetry sales to survive on. Visit the website at *www.lummoxpress.com/lc* for ordering a book or two and help the guy out!

Austin Alexis is the author of *Privacy Issues* (Broadside Lotus Pres, Detroit, 2014) and two previously published chapbooks of poetry.

His fiction, poetry and reviews have appeared in *Barrow Street, The Journal, Paterson Literary Review, Point of View Magazine, LUMMOX Anthology*, the anthology *Suitcase of Chrysanthemums* (Great Weather for Media Press) and elsewhere.

Karen Basiulis is retired after a long career in project and contracts management, mostly in the aerospace industry. She holds a Bachelor of Music degree in Voice from Cal State Long Beach, and a Master of Science degree in Systems Management from USC. Her passions are singing and poetry, both of which had to take a back seat during her career, but are now important parts of her life again. She lives in San Pedro with her husband and two semi-feral cats.

Brenton Booth lives in Sydney, Australia. His book BASH THE KEYS UNTIL THEY SCREAM is available from Epic Rites Press.

Ann Bracken, an activist with a pen, has authored two poetry collections, *No Barking in the Hallways: Poems from the Classroom and The Altar of Innocence*, serves as a contributing editor for *Little Patuxent Review,* and co-facilitates the Wilde Readings Poetry Series. Her poetry, essays, and interviews have appeared in anthologies and journals, including *Women Write Resistance, Mad in America, Fledgling Rag*, and *Gargoyle*. Ann's poetry has garnered two Pushcart Prize nominations and her advocacy work centers around arts-based interventions for mental health, education, and prison reform. Website: *www.annbrackenauthor.com*

Debbi Brody conducts poetry workshops and readings at festivals and other venues throughout the Southwest to writers age five through eighty-

REAL ESTATE

Local Expertise ~ International Network ~ Personalized Service

Andrea Kowalski, Golden West Realty
1517 S. Gaffey St. San Pedro, CA BRE#00856244
Realtor®, CNE®, SRES®
BRE#01380823

Phone: 310-433-3349
www.AndreaK.com

"I've known Andrea since the early 90s and I've always admired her dedication and work ethic. I wouldn't hesitate to recommend her to any of my friends." -RD Armstrong

five. Her work appears in many international, national and regional magazines, journals, and books of note including numerous anthologies. Her latest award winning book, *In Everything Birds,* (Village Books Press, Oklahoma, 2015), as well as her most recent chapbook, *"Walking the Arroyo,"* are available through artqueen58@aol.com for signed copies and through the usual online purchase sources. Debbi lives in Santa Fe where she works for a small R&D company and where she is still revising that next darn full-length manuscript..

Lynne Bronstein is celebrating numerous decades of being involved in poetry. She has published four books, with a fifth book to come out one of these days. Her poetry and short fiction have appeared in everything from Playgirl to Chiron Review, from underground newspapers to National Public Radio. Her poetry videos are on her own YouTube channel. She lives in the San Fernando Valley with two humans, three cats, and a Beta fish.

Montana poet **B.J. Buckley** grew up in Cheyenne, Wyoming, across the street from Lakeview Cemetary, where she played with her Barbies on mausoleum steps, buried dead birds, and kept lists of names from gravestones to use for characters in future stories.

April Bulmer is an award-winning Canadian poet. She has a dozen books published. Her work has appeared in many prestigious journals such as *The Malahat Review, PRISM international* and *Journal of Feminist Studies in Religion.* April holds three Master's degrees in creative writing and religious studies. She lives in Cambridge, Ontario where she was recently awarded the Cambridge YWCA Women of Distinction Award in their Arts & Culture category. Her most recent manuscript was shortlisted for the international Beverly Prize in London, England, held by Eyewear Publishing. Her book of poetry called *Out of Darkness, Light* (Hidden Brook Press, John B.

Lee Signature Series) was a finalist in the 2019 Next Generation Indie Book Awards in their spirituality category. It is available from April at *april.poet@bell.net.*

Wayne F. Burke's poetry has been published in a wide variety of publications online and in print (including LUMMOX Anthology). He is the author of seven full-length poetry collections--most recently ESCAPE FROM THE PLANET CROUTON (Luchador Press, 2019). He lives in the central Vermont area, USA.

Helmut C. Calabrese, PhD, the Italian-American born in Germany, lived in the village of Bocholt until the age of five. The Calabrese family immigrated in 1962 to Philadelphia, Pennsylvania. At the age of ten, Helmut began studying "the black and white ivories" with a private tutor of the piano. On the advice of his English teacher, he began writing poetry after graduating high school. Helmut met David Roskos, the publisher of Iniquity Press/Vendetta Books in 2017 and had his first book of poetry, *New Creation: Collected Poems Of Helmut Christoferus Calabrese 1975-2019* published.

Don Kingfisher Campbell, MFA in Creative Writing from Antioch University Los Angeles, has taught Writers Seminar at Occidental College Upward Bound for 35 years, been a coach and judge for Poetry Out Loud, a performing poet/teacher for Red Hen Press Youth Writing Workshops, L.A. Coordinator and Board Member of California Poets In The Schools, poetry editor of the Angel City Review, publisher of Spectrum magazine, and host of the Saturday Afternoon Poetry reading series in Pasadena, California. For awards, features, and publication credits, please go to: *http://dkc1031.blogspot.com*

The poems of **Pris Campbell** have appeared in numerous journals and anthologines. Nominated six times for a Pushcart, the Small Press has published eight collections of her poetry. *My*

Southern Childhood, from Nixes Mate Press is her most recent book. A former Clinical Psychologist, sailor and bicyclist until sidelined by ME/CFS, a neuroimmune illness, in 1990, she makes her home with her husband in the Greater West Palm Beach, Florida.

Dominican-American poet **Luís Campos** was present when the Venice Poetry Workshop first met on a summer Wednesday evening in 1969. Won first prize in the Bay Area Coalition Contest of 1983; also the Unknown Reader Award of Electrum Magazine in 1987. His poem "A North Hollywood Ending" was recently published in The New York Times.

Alan Catlin is the author of *Last Man Standing* published by LUMMOX Press. He has two new full length books out in 2020: *Asylum Garden: after Van Gogh* from Dos Madres and *Lessons in Darkness* from Luchador Press.

Grace Cavalieri is Maryland's tenth Poet Laureate. She's the author of 26 books and chapbooks of poetry and 20 short-form and full-length plays. *What The Psychic Said* is her new publication (Goss Publications, 2020.) The previous book of poems is *Showboat,* (Goss publications 2019,) about 25 years as a Navy wife. Her latest play "Quilting The Sun" was produced at the Theater for the New City, NYC in 2019. She founded and produces "the Poet and the Poem" for public radio, now from the Library of Congress, celebrating 43 years on-air.

Jackie Chou is a poet residing in sunny Southern California. She likes to identify as neurodivergent as she has battled bipolar disorder most of her adult life and writes about her experience with mental illness. She writes about other topics as well. She has been published in LUMMOX, Altadena Poetry Review, JOMP 21 Dear Mr President anthology, Creative Talents Unleashed anthologies, and others.

Jonathan Church is an economist, CFA charter holder, and writer who has been published in Areo, Quillette, Arc Digital, The Agonist Journal, Merion West, DC Examiner, Big Hammer, Street Value, LUMMOX, The Good Men Project, and other venues.

Coco – Author of Unicorn Psychosis, is Spectrum Publishing's Historian, Pasadena poet, and mental health advocate. Her work is born of trauma while overcoming medical impossibilities. Published in LUMMOX 8, the Altadena Poetry Review (2019), Spectrum, Animal Heart Press and Fall 2019 INSCAPE Director of Operations – Chief Consulting Editor. Coco loves being a mother and mentor to her two amazing boys.

Ed Coletti is a poet, painter, fiction writer and middling chess player. Previously, he served for three years as an Army Officer, then as a Counselor and later as a Small Business Consultant. Recent poems have appeared in *ZYZZYVA, North American Review, Volt, Spillway,* and *Blueline.* Most recent poetry collections include *The Problem With Breathing (Edwin Smith Publishing* –Little Rock- 2015) and *Apollo Blue's Harp And The Gods Of Song* published by *McCaa Books* February 2019. He lives with his wife Joyce in Santa Rosa, California. Ed also curates a popular ten-year-old blog "No Money In Poetry" *http:// edwardcolettispoetryblog.blogspot.com/*

Sharyl Collin's poems have appeared in various publications including *Switched-On Gutenberg, Waypoints, The Intentional, Wild Goose Poetry, Mason's Road Literary Journal, *82 Review, Mothers Always Write* and *LUMMOX.* She is excited to co-host the Poetry Apocalypse open mic with Linda Singer on the third Sundays of each month at Angel's Gate Cultural Center in San Pedro. Sharyl also enjoys photography and playing her guitar.

Beverly M. Collins is the Author of the books,

Quiet Observations: Diary thought, Whimsy and Rhyme and *Mud in Magic*. Her works have also appeared in California Quarterly, Poetry Speaks! A year of Great Poems and Poets, The Hidden and the Divine Female Voices in Ireland, The Journal of Modern Poetry, Spectrum, LUMMOX, The Galway Review (Ireland), Verse of Silence (New Delhi), Peeking Cat Poetry Magazine (London), Scarlet Leaf Review (Canada), The Wild Word magazine (Berlin), Indigomania (Australia) and many others.

Pat Connors chapbook, *Scarborough Songs*, was published by Lyricalmyrical Press in 2013, and charted on the Toronto Poetry Map. *Part-Time Contemplative*, his second chapbook with Lyricalmyrical, was released in 2016. Other publication credits include: Spadina Literary Review; The Toronto Quarterly; and *Tamaracks*, an anthology of Canadian poets released last spring in Long Beach, California. His first full collection is forthcoming.

Henry Crawford's work appears frequently in journals and online publications. He has two collections of poetry: American Software and The Binary Planet. His poem The Fruits of Famine, won first prize in the 2019 World Food Poetry Competition. He volunteers in the DC poetry community, serving as MC and/or co-director for The Word Works Cafe Muse Literary Salon, the Joaquin Miller Poetry Series, A Splendid Wake and is MC for the online poetry series Poets vs The Pandemic. His website is *HenryCrawfordPoetry.com*.

Chris Cressey enjoys a very full life with her son, daughter in law and granddaughter on a shared property in Altadena. She began her writing in earnest after a move from Malibu in 2016. Her work has been published in *The Nasty Women's Almanac*, Spectrum and *The Altadena Literary Review* (2020). Chris also enjoys gardening, cooking, hiking, and entertaining friends.

Joel Dailey lives in New Orleans.

Michael Estabrook is retired and writing more poems and working more outside; just noticed two Cooper's hawks staked out in the yard or rather above it which explains the nerve-wracked chipmunks. *The Poet's Curse, A Miscellany* (The Poetry Box, 2019) is a recent collection.

Mark Evans was born in Kansas (1954) and has lived in various cities throughout California. After high school (Los Angeles, CA), Mark entered a two-year Liberal Arts curriculum at Los Angeles Harbor Jr. College. Mark's passion is music and lyric, but recently found poetry to be a powerfully expressive niche. He is the author of a notable book: *Hotel Linen* [2015], and has recently published his latest work of poetry, entitled: *The Dogs Behind the Fence*, which was released in June 2018. He is currently an expat residing in Portugal.

Alexis Rhone Fancher is published in *Best American Poetry, Rattle, Hobart, Verse Daily, Plume, Cleaver, Diode, Poetry East, Flock, Duende, Nashville Review, Pedestal Magazine* and elsewhere. She's authored five poetry collections, most recently, *Junkie Wife (Moon Tide Press, 2018)*, and *The Dead Kid Poems (KYSO Flash Press, 2019).* Her 6th collection, *EROTIC: New & Selected*, publishes in August 2020 from New York Quarterly, and another full-length collection (in Italian) will be published in 2021 by Edizioni Ensemble, Italia. Her photographs are featured worldwide. A multiple Pushcart Prize and Best of the Net nominee, Alexis is poetry editor of *Cultural Weekly. www.alexisrhonefancher.com*

Joseph Farley edited *Axe Factory* from 1986 to 2010. His poetry books include *Suckers*, Cynic Press, 2004, and *Longing for the Mother Tongue*, March Street Press, 2010. His chapbooks include *January*, Philadelphia Poetry Project, 1986, and *Her Eyes*, Ygdrasil,

2012. His fiction works include *For the Birds,* Cynic Press, 2001, and *Labor Day,* Peasantry Press, 2016, reissued in a special edition in 2019. His work has appeared recently in Wilderness House Review, Home Planet New Online, Horror Sleaze Trash, Schlock!, Mad Swirl, US 1 Worksheets, Big Windows and other places.

Sarah Ferris is published in RATTLE, Ol'Shanty, and Ascent Aspirations. Her chapbook, *Snakes That Dance Like Daffodils,* was published April, 2019. A novel is in the works. Sarah has an MA in Spiritual Psychology from the University of Santa Monica, and a BA in Cinema Studies from NYU. She lives in Los Angeles with her family.

This is **Gwendolyn Fleischer's** 2nd time in a LUMMOX publication. She has also been published in the Palos Verdes Anthology and Spectrum. Currently she is sheltering in place and zooming and can't wait to get back to live events.

Dennis Formento a poet and activist lives in Slidell, LA, across Lake Pontchartrain from his native New Orleans. St. Tammany Parish co-ordinator of 100,000 Poets for Change. Author of *Spirit Vessels* (FootHills Publishing, 2018), Cineplex (Paper Press, 2014,) *Looking for An Out Place* (FootHills Publishing, 2010.) Edited *Mesechabe: The Journal of Surregionalism* and founded Surregional Press. Some of his poems have even been translated into Italian, & just today arrived "Amarcord," in *Americans and Others: International Poetry Anthology*, ed. Giulio Tedeschi, Camion Press.

Bill Gainer is a storyteller, a humorist and an award winning poet. His BA is from St. Mary's College and his MPA from USF. He is the publisher of the PEN Award winning R. L. Crow Publications. Gainer is internationally published and known across the country for giving legendary fun filled performances. His latest book is *The Mysterious Book of old Man*

Poems. Visit him in his books, at his personal appearances, or at his website: *billgainer.com.*

William Scott Galasso is the author of sixteen books of poetry including *Mixed Bag,* (A Travelogue in Four Forms), 2018, and *Rough Cut: Thirty Years of Senryu* (2019) available on Amazon. In addition, he edited *Eclipse Moon,* (2017), the 20th Anniversary issue. *Thirty Years of Haiku,* is due out in fall of 2020 (Galwin Press), also on Amazon.

Martina Gallegos came to California from Mexico before her fifteenth birthday and spoke no English. She attended high school through graduate school. She was a bilingual teacher for eighteen years. She suffered a work injury and subsequent stroke; she returned to school after her stroke and got her Master's degree in 2015. Her work has appeared in Silver Birch Press, Hometown Pasadena, SGVQR, Poets Responding, LUMMOX, APR, Spirit Fire Review, Poetry SuperHighway, Central Coast Poetry Shows, and others. She has a daughter, a lovebird, and her cat Estrellita. They live in Oxnard, CA.

J.W. Gardner is a poet from East Lakewood, CA. He was the creator and producer of The Last Sunday, a congressionally recognized monthly poetry reading, along with being published in multiple anthologies. His first book, *In The Shadow Of The Bomb* can be found at LUMMOX Press.

Tony Gloeggler is a life-long resident of New York City and has managed group homes for the mentally challenged in Brooklyn for 40 years. His work has appeared in Rattle, Nerve Cowboy. New Ohio Review, Spillway, Trailer Park Quarterly and Black Coffee Review. His full length books include *One Wish Left* (Pavement Saw Press 2002) and *Until The Last Light Leaves* (NYQ Books 2015). His next book will be published by NYQ Books in 2020

Kathleen Goldman A long time South Bay resident, Kathleen lives and writes in Manhattan Beach. Her background in journalism taught her to keep it brief which she sometimes succeeds in doing. Her book, *Down River*, came out in 2014. She's putting finishing touches on a new chapbook that she'd love to see in print by this time next year.

Art Goodtimes, newspaper columnist, Telluride Institute fellow and Rainbow Family elder, weaves non-traditional coil baskets and grows organic heirloom seed potatoes, He served as Poet Laureate of Colorado's Western Slope (2011-13) and retired in 2017 after 20 years as Colorado's only Green Party county commissioner. His most recent book is *Dancing on Edge: the McRedeye Poems* (Lithic Press, Fruita, 2019).

Katherine L. Gordon is a rural Ontario poet humbled and inspired by the wonders of nature in her secluded river valley. She has books, chapbooks, essays and reviews published internationally. Her latest book "Landscapes" a collaboration with James Deahl, her latest collection Piping at the End of Days. Working with fine contemporaries is the vitality of life.

Tony Gruenewald is the author of *The Secret History of New Jersey* (Northwind). More at *tonygruenewald.com*.

Tom Gannon Hamilton, author, painter, career musician, was awarded first prize in the 2018 Big Pond Rumours Chapbook Competition for the poem suite *El Marillo* and his major collection *Panoptic* (Aeolus House 2018) won critical acclaim (see opusonereview.com) His forthcoming book, *The Mezzo Soprano Dines Alone*, is featured in the John B Lee Signature Series (2020).

For the past twenty-five years, **Vijali Hamilton** has worked and taught around the world as an artist/peacemaker. She collaborates with diversified communities and utilizes her skills as a sculptor, filmmaker, poet, musician, and author. Vijali started her World Wheel Project in 1986 to further explore the role that community-based art can play in building a world at peace. Vijali spent ten years as a monastic member of the Vedanta Society convent in Santa Barbara. She gives seminars and retreats on meditation and the creative process, internationally and at her World Wheel Center outside of Santa Fe, New Mexico.

Charles Harmon loves to write, loves to live, loves to love, loves to cook, loves to eat. Teaching science is like cooking, cooking is like writing poetry, poetry is about life, love is about living and living is being in love. Long live poetry, life, and love! Enjoys cooking for his family and friends, writing poetry and stories and songs. Currently working on a novel.

Michael Hathaway lives in the middle of Kansas with his clowder of "little lions and tiny tigers." By day, he works as Keeper of History for Stafford County, and by night edits and publishes *Chiron Review* literary journal which he founded in 1982. His latest books are *Talking to Squirrels* and *Postmarked Home: New & Selected Poems 1979-2019*, both published in 2019 by Spartan Press, and available at Amazon and Barnes & Noble.

George Held has won several haiku awards, including a blue ribbon at the 2019 Long Island state fair. His latest poetry collection is *Second Sight* (Poets Wear Prada, 2019).

Debbie Okun Hill is a Canadian poet who gardens words full-time in rural southwestern Ontario. To date, over 435 of her poems have been published in publications/e-zines including *LUMMOX, TAMARACKS, Mobius, Still Point Arts Quarterly, The Binnacle, THEMA* and *Phati'tude Literary Magazine* in the United States. She has one trade book published by Black Moss Press and four award-winning

A DIVISON OF LUMMOX PRODUCTIONS

MOON IN THE BUCKET FUND

One man's effort to help those who have been abandoned by society

562 331-4351   poetraindog@gmail.com

chapbooks. She blogs about literary happenings including LUMMOX's Canadian launches at *http://okunhill.wordpress.com/*

Gil Hagen Hill was born in Culver City, California. He has been published in numerous small press venues.He received a BA in Theater Arts from C.S.U.L.A. in 1973.He is a member of Poetry Apocalypse. He is a frequent contributor to LUMMOX Press, who his Chapbook *Circle of Bones* (2018 LUMMOX Press).

Lori Wall-Holloway is a wife, mother and proud grandmother of nine grandchildren, resides in the San Gabriel Valley. Her poetry has appeared in various publications throughout the years, but more recently it has been included in the Spectrum anthologies, LUMMOX editions 7 and 8 as well as the 2015-2020 publications of the Altadena Poetry Review.

Rehanul Hoque was born in a village of Bangladesh, Rehanul, a bilingual poet, is a worshiper of beauty and wants to promote beauty and truth together through the appreciation of beauty, by means of poetry. He dreams of a future ruled only by love.

Ilhem Issaoui is a Tunisian researcher, poet, and translator. She has been published in many countries including the US, the UK, Canada, and India in print and online. She is in the process of publishing her second poetry collection.

M.J. Iuppa's fourth poetry collection is *This Thirst* (Kelsay Books, 2017). For the past 31 years, she has lived on a small farm near the shores of Lake Ontario. Check out her blog: *mjiuppa.blogspot.com* for her musings on writing, sustainability & life's stew.

Ed Jamieson has been published in various magazines: California Pop, Night, Bender, Nerve Cowboy, LUMMOX Journal, Voices of the Library, and Poesy.

Diane Klammer is a poet, songwriter, mental health counselor and naturalist living in Boulder, Colorado. She believes that when your health goes, everything else is superfluous, don't mind the pun. She has a giant blog and one published book, but just loves to write and does it for free.

Frank Kearns is a transplanted New Englander and a longtime California resident. He is the author of three poetry collections, *Circling Venice* (2013), *Yearlings* (2015), and *Pleasant Street* (2019). His work has also appeared in anthologies such as *Beyond the Lyric Moment, Like a Girl: Perspectives on Feminism, The California Writers Club Literary Review* and in an upcoming edition of *Sand Canyon Review.*

R.J. Keeler was born St. Paul, Minnesota, grew up in jungles of Colombia. BS Mathematics North Carolina State University, MS Computer Science University of North Carolina-Chapel Hill, MBA University of California at Los Angeles, and Certificate in Poetry University of Washington. Honorman in the U.S. Naval Submarine School and Submarine Service (SS) qualified. Recipient of the Vietnam Service Medal, Honorable Discharge, and Whiting Foundation Experimental Grant. Member of IEEE, AAAS, Academy of American Poets. A former Boeing engineer.

Jesse James Kennedy is an American novelist and poet born in St. Louis Missouri. After a brief stint in the Army, he spent a good decade running wild, reading and sharpening his writing skills. His first novel, *MISSOURI HOMEGROWN*, was published by Perfect Crime Books to strong national reviews from Publishers Weekly and Booklist. His second novel, *TIJUANA MEAN*, was accepted by the same publisher and received a strong national Review from Booklist. He's had poems included in the international anthology, *YEARINGS* and a short horror story in the Halloween anthology *HOUSE OF HORRORS 2* by Alien Buddha Press.

lalo kikiriki was once Mandy Pression of KPFT in Houston, once Ms. Palmer-Lacy of LAUSD, once Jenifer Palmer-Lacy, instigator and curator of The Celebration in Runyon Canyon. lalo, who has published many oddball poems in the journals and 3 chapbooks including *Dreams of the Everyday Housewife*, is currently distancing in Joshua Tree.

Doug Knott has been writing and performing poetry in Southern California for many years. He is the author of the collection, *Small Dogs Bark Cartoons*, various chapbooks, and is included in the anthology, *Outlaw Poetry Bible.* He was a member of the poetry-performance troupe the Carma Bums, and was the president of the board of Beyond Baroque Literary Foundation 2013-2017. He is a lifelong student and fan of the "Beat Generation" and is delighted to publish with LUMMOX for that reason.

Jacqueline Kras Pinson is a poet and visual artist living and working in North Hollywood, CA. She earned her BFA in Painting and Drawing from CSULB in 2000 and has lived in Southern California for the majority of her life. She is a Professional Organizer, mother of one son, and an amateur archer.

Tom Laichas's work appeared in *LUMMOX 7* (2018). His recent work has appeared or is forthcoming in *Ambit, Spillway, Masque & Spectacle, Altadena Review* and elsewhere.

His debut collection, *Empire of Eden* is now available from The High Window Press. A chapbook, *Sixty-Three Photographs from the End of a War,* will be released later this year by 3.1 Venice Press.

Michou Landon is a poet and a mystic currently caught in the orbit of Santa Fe, NM, USA. At this writing she is living (and taking notes for) a novel: *Love in the Time of Corona.* She occasionally posts a blog at *taodaughter. wordpress.com.*

Donna Langevin's latest poetry collections include *The Laundress of Time*, Aeolus House 2014 and *Brimming*, Piquant Press 2019. She won second prize in the 2017 Banister Anthology Competition, and first prize in 2019. Her plays, *the Dinner* and *Bargains in the New World* won first prizes for script at the Eden Mills Festival in 2014 and 2015. *If Socrates Were in My Shoes* was produced at the Alumnae Theatre NIF Festival in 2018 and *Remember Him Chasing Squirrels* was performed there in 2020. She looks forward to the publication of *The Summer of Saints*, her poem/play about the 1848 typhus epidemic by Prometea Press.

Laura Muñoz-Larbig received a Bachelor's Degree in English with an Emphasis in Creative Writing from California State University in 1980. In 2002, she earned a Preliminary Adult Education Credential in English, and worked as a substitute teacher. Her writing degree fulfilled a lifelong passion with the writing craft that began when she was 11 years old. Both poetry and prose were published in anthologies and Opinion Editorials in newspapers, from the 1970s to the present. Poems and two essays were published in LUMMOX Numbers 2-4 and 6-8 (2013 through 2019), and in Psalms of Cinder and Silt (2019).

Kyle Laws is based out of the Arts Alliance Studios Community in Pueblo, CO where she directs Line/Circle: Women Poets in

Performance. Her collections include *Ride the Pink Horse* (Stubborn Mule Press, 2019), *Faces of Fishing Creek* (Middle Creek Publishing, 2018), *This Town: Poems of Correspondence* with Jared Smith (Liquid Light Press, 2017), *So Bright to Blind* (Five Oaks Press, 2015), and *Wildwood* (LUMMOX Press, 2014). With eight nominations for a Pushcart Prize, her poems and essays have appeared in magazines and anthologies in the U.S., U.K., Canada, and Germany. She is the editor and publisher of Casa de Cinco Hermanas Press.

Marie Lecrivain is a poet, publisher of *poeticdiversity: the litzine of Los Angeles*, and ordained priestess in the Ecclesia Gnostica Catholica, the ecclesiastical arm of Ordo Templi Orientis. Her work has been published in *Nonbinary Review, Orbis, Pirene's Fountain*, and many other journals. She's the author of several books of poetry and fiction, and editor of *Gondal Heights: A Bronte Tribute Anthology* (copyright 2019 Sybaritic Press, *www.sybpress.com*)

John B. Lee is a recipient of the Canada 150 Medal for his outstanding contribution to literature, he was also presented with the Dogwood Award in recognition of his contribution to culture and heritage in his home county and in the autumn of 2020 he will receive the Arthur Lefebvre Award for Excellence in Career Achievement. He lives in a lake house overlooking Long Point Bay where he works as a full-time writer and editor. John B. Lee's latest book *Darling, May I Touch Your Pinkletink* is forthcoming from Hidden Brook Press in 2020.

Rick Leddy is a cartoonist, poet and author. His poems have appeared in the Spectrum, Intersections, Altadena Poetry Review and LUMMOX #8 poetry anthologies. He has published two poetry collections: Metro Mona Lisa and 365+1: A Year of Beauty and Madness.

Linda Lerner's recent collection is, When Death is a Red Balloon, (LUMMOX Press, 2019). Previously published, A Dance Around the Cauldron, a prose work which consists of nine characters during the Salem witch trials brought into our own times (LUMMOX Press, 2017). Yes, the Ducks Were Real & Takes Guts and Years Sometimes (NYQ Books (2011 & 2015). Current publications include, Maintenant, Gargoyle, Paterson Literary Review, Café Review, Trailer Park Quarterly, Wilderness Literary House Review, Cape Rock, Piker Press, Home Planet New, etc. In spring, 2015 she read six poems on WBAI. Taking the F train was accepted by NYQ books for future publication

Jane Lipman's first full-length poetry collection, *On the Back Porch of the Moon*, Black Swan Editions, 2012, won the 2013 NM/AZ Award and a 2013 NM Press Women's Award. Her chapbooks, *The Rapture of Tulips* and *White Crow's Secret Life*, Pudding House Publications, 2009, were finalists for NM Book Awards in Poetry in 2009 and 2010, respectively. During the '80s she founded and directed Taos Institute, which sponsored performances and workshops by Robert Bly, Joseph Campbell, Gioia Timpanelli, Paul Winter, and others.

Ellaraine Lockie's recent poems have won the 2019 Poetry Super Highway Contest, the Nebraska Writers Guild's Women of the Fur Trade Poetry Contest and New Millennium's Monthly Musepaper Poetry Contest. Her fourteenth chapbook, *Sex and Other Slapsticks*, was recently released from Presa Press. Earlier collections have won Poetry Forum's Chapbook Contest Prize, San Gabriel Valley Poetry Festival Chapbook Competition, Encircle Publications Chapbook Contest, Best Individual Poetry Collection Award from Purple Patch magazine in England, and The Aurorean's Chapbook Choice Award. Ellaraine also teaches writing workshops and serves as Poetry Editor for the lifestyles magazine, LILIPOH.

Radomir Vojtech Luza was born in Vienna, Austria in 1963 to renowned Czech parents. The SAG/AFTRA/AEA union actor is The Poet Laureate of North Hollywood, CA, a Pushcart Prize nominee and the author of 30 books (26 collections of poetry) of which the latest poetry collection, SIDEWALKS AND STREET CORNERS, was published by Christian Faith Publishing in 2018. The veteran stand-up comedian has been penning poems for 33 years. He has had nearly 100 poems published in literary journals, anthologies, websites, newspapers, magazines and other media. To Luza, poetry is the literary bridge to God.

Argos MacCallum is an actor, director, carpenter, theatre manager, and co-founder of Teatro Paraguas, a bilingual theatre company promoting Latinx plays in Santa Fe, New Mexico. He has lived the past 50 years in his homestead in the shadow of the Cerrillos Hills off the Turquoise Trail outside Santa Fe, where the coyotes party all night long.

John Macker's latest books are *The Blues Drink Your Dreams Away Selected Poems 1983-2018* (finalist for the Arizona/New Mexico Book Award) and *Atlas of Wolves*. Upcoming: *El Rialto*, a chapbook with serigraphs by Leon Loughridge.

Mike Mahoney was born in Wallingford with a mushroom-shaped left hip, Mahoney kills time giving birth to Art on the cave walls of his Imagination while he waits for the rest of the world to wake up. He's a firm believer in the written word over the meme, the typewritten over the digital. He agrees with Albert Huffstickler that the real revolution will be about feelings & perceptions, not about governments & killing people.

DS Maolalai has been nominated four times for Best of the Net and three times for the Pushcart Prize. His poetry has been released in

two collections, *"Love is Breaking Plates in the Garden"* (Encircle Press, 2016) and *"Sad Havoc Among the Birds"* (Turas Press, 2019).

Adrian Manning lives and writes from Leicester, England. He has had a number of chapbooks and broadsides published. His latest book is a full length collection of selected poems called 'Digging Up The Bones' published by Uncollected Press in the USA. He is also the editor of Concrete Meat Press.

Georiga Santa Maria is a Native New Mexican, and is an artist, photographer and writer. She has been published in many anthologies. Her books *LichenKisses*, 2013, *Dowsing* (LUMMOX Press, 2017), *Berlin Poems and Photographs* (2017), co-written with Merimée Moffitt, and *The My Ami Hippie Mommy Cookbook* (2019) are available. She was the recipient of the LUMMOX Poetry Prize in 2016, and a First Place winner in 2018 with New Mexico Press Women for "Photography with Related Text," for *Berlin Poems and Photographs,* and an Honorable mention for the same from The National Federation of Press Women.

Richard Martin's most recent books of poetry are *Techniques in the Neighborhood of Sleep* (Spuyten Duyvil, 2016), *Goosebumps of Antimatter* (Spuyten Duyvil, 2018), and *Hard Labor* (Igneus Press, 2019) His latest book of poetry, *Ceremony of the Unknown*, will be available from Spuyten Duyvil Press in the summer (2020).

Michael M. Meloan's work has appeared in Wired, Huffington Post, Buzz, LA Weekly, and in a variety of anthologies including LUMMOX Press. He was an interview subject in the documentaries "Bukowski: Born Into This" and "Joe Frank: Somewhere Out There." With Joe Frank, he co-wrote a number of radio shows that aired across the NPR syndicate. His Wired short story "The Cutting Edge" was optioned twice for film. And he co-authored the novel "The Shroud" with his brother Steven.

Mary McGinnis, blind since birth, has been writing and living in New Mexico since 1972 where she has connected with emptiness, desert, and mountains. Published in over 80 magazines and anthologies, she has been nominated for a Pushcart Prize, and has three full length collections: *Listening for Cactus* (1996), *October Again* (2008), *See with Your Whole Body* (2016), and a chapbook, *Breath of Willow*, published by LUMMOX for winning the poetry contest in 2017. Mary frequently offers poetry readings and writing workshops.

As poetry rarely pays well, **David McIntire** (he/him) has taken on numerous occupations over the years including printer, flooring installer, delivery boy, factotum, retail manager, warehouse worker, pharmacy technician, security guard, handyman, Uber driver and roadie. He lives in the Poetry Bus in Portland, Oregon. His latest collection, *Everything I Write is a Love Song to the World* was published last year by Moon Tide Press while his first two books of poetry, *Punk Rock Breakfast* and *No One Will Believe You* were published by International Word Bank Press.

Basia Miller's poems have appeared in *Trickster, LUMMOX, Malpais Review*, and the *Santa Fe Literary Review* as well as in the French poetry journals *Poésie-sur-Seine* and *Portulan bleu*. Her first chapbook, *The Next Village/Le prochain village*, was self-published in 2016. Her second chapbook is *Backyard Tree/ L'Arbre côté cour* (Paris : D'Ici et D'Ailleurs, Collection « Les Intuitistes, » 2017). Her translations have appeared in collector's editions of poetry combined with art, including "Cantate pour le Grand Canyon," by Francine Caron with linocuts by Pierre Cayol (Transignum, 2009) and "Le Chant de Naatsis'aan," by Marie Cayol (Imprimeries du Gard Rhodanien, 2011).

Joe Milosch graduated from San Diego State University. His poetry has appeared in various magazines, including the California Quarterly. He has multiple nominations for the Pushcart and received the Hackney Award for Literature. His books: *The Lost Pilgrimage Poems, Landscape of a Hummingbird*, and *Homeplate Was the Heart*. He worked as a trail locator for the Cleveland National Forest and draws inspiration from that job as well as his experiences growing up in the farmland, north of Detroit, Michigan and his army experiences during the Vietnam War.

Tony Moffeit was the director of the Pueblo, Colorado Poetry Project for forty years. He is the recipient of a National Endowment for the Arts creative writing fellowship, the Jack Kerouac Award, and the Denver Press Club's Thomas Hornsby Ferril Poetry Prize. He performed his poetry and songs with blues guitarist Rick Terlep. His *Born to be Blue*, LUMMOX Press, was a finalist for Colorado Book Award.

Bill Mohr lives in Long Beach. He teaches at CSULB. Not much else is known about him except he is an awfully nice guy. Oh yeah, recently he's gotten into painting.

Robert A. Morris lives near Baton Rouge and works as a teacher. Besides poetry, he also writes fiction and bashes out the occasional song on his blue Stratocaster. A recent poem of his has been selected to appear in a future issue of *As It Ought to Be Magazine*. His work has appeared in *The Main Street Rag, Pear Noir*, and *The Chaffin Review* among others. *https:// robertamorrisblog.wordpress.com*

Evan "Mikey" Myquest is a poet, writer, and Cubs fan married for 44 years to his Swiss-German wife, Eva. They live near Sacramento, CA and are known for being café art and music patrons. Myquest was born in North Central Illinois, grew up on the pulp science fiction and mystery magazines of the 60s. His poetry has appeared alongside Leonard Cohen, Lawrence Ferlinghetti, Jack Hirschman, Patti Smith, Jim Carroll, and Ann Menebroker. In 2017, a tribute documentary video by Susana Halfon featuring his poetry was premiered at the Crocker Art Museum in Sacramento. His daughter Alicia still resides in northern Illinois.

Linda Neal lives with her dog, Mantra, near the beach. She studied literature at Pomona College and later earned a BA in linguistics and an MA in clinical psychology. She was a practicing therapist for three decades. She holds an MFA in poetry from Pacific University. Her poems have appeared or are forthcoming in numerous journals, including *Calyx, Chiron Review, Crack the Spine, LUMMOX, Prairie Schooner, Santa Fe Literary Review* and *Tampa Review*. She has won awards from Beyond Baroque Foundation, Pacific Coast Journal and PEN Women Writers. *Dodge & Burn*, her first collection came out in 2014. *Not About Dinosaurs* will be out in the summer of 2020.

Since 1979, Detroit-born **Joseph Nicks** has divided his waking hours more-or-less equally between his "day job" and his nocturnal writing. The diurnal component has varied from manual laborer to water quality lab technician, assistant science advisor to a museum exhibits development team, technical writer, public school biology teacher, and field biologist. He holds a B.S. in terrestrial zoology and two teaching credentials (multiple subject and single subject-biology) and currently lives in the Mojave Desert. Recent publications include *Tales From The Otherground* (2014), *Songs From The Dirt* (2015) and *Can't Forget The Motor City...* (2018).

Tom Obrzut is a New Jersey poet and one of the founders and editors of Arbella Magazine. He has had a variety of jobs primarily working with homeless, mentally ill people in need of housing. Tom has been published in Big Hammer, Long Shot, Poetry Motel, and by Alien Buddha Press. His recent book of poems "Street Life" was published by Iniquity Press / Vendetta Books and is available on Amazon. He is one of the organizers of the Poets Wednesday series at the Barron Arts Center, Woodbridge, NJ. He currently works in a psychiatric unit in Elizabeth, NJ.

Norman Olson is a small press poet and artist in Maplewood, Minnesota. He has published hundreds of poems and drawings and his book, 44 Image Poems is available at: *http://www.lulu. com/shop/norman-j-olson/forty-four-image-poems/paperback/product-23723310.html*.

Dean Okamura lives in Torrance. He enjoys writing everyday stories. To Dean, personal memories are helpful, familiar faces in a crowd. Dean's interest in his family's roots led him to Japan in 2017 for a discovery visit.

Scott Thomas Outlar lives and writes in the suburbs outside of Atlanta, Georgia. His work has been nominated for the Pushcart Prize and Best of the Net. Selections of his poetry have been translated into Afrikaans, Albanian, Bengali, Dutch, French, Italian, Kurdish, Persian, Serbian, and Spanish. His sixth book, *Of Sand and Sugar*, was released in 2019 through Cyberwit Press. He hosts a podcast, Songs of Selah, that airs weekly on 17Numa Radio and features interviews with contemporary poets, artists, musicians, and health advocates. More about Outlar's work can be found at *17Numa.com*.

Lorine Parks progenitor of Catalina Eddy and Persons of Interest, curates a weekly Poetry Matters column for The Downey Patriot. For six years from 2012 to 2018 on behalf of the Downey Arts Coalition, she hosted a monthly poetry reading in Downey, including all of LUMMOX's annual book launches, showcasing guest artists and local poets at venues ranging from Mari's Wine Bar and the Rives Mansion to The Epic Lounge and Stay Gallery.

Simon Perchik is an attorney whose poems have appeared in *Partisan Review, Forge, Poetry, Osiris, The New Yorker* and elsewhere. His most recent collection is *The Rosenblum Poems* published by *Cholla Needles Arts & Literary Library*, 2020. For more information including free e-books and his essay "Magic, Illusion and Other Realities" please visit his website at *www.simonperchik.com.*

Jeannine Pitas lives, writes, teaches and translates in Dubuque, Iowa. If you liked her poem in this issue, then you should purchase and read her chapbook, *thank you for dreaming*, which was published by LUMMOX Press in 2018. She has since done other chaps and has a full collection coming out soon.

Charles Plymell *www.washburn.edu/reference/cks/mapping/plymell/index.html* or *http://www.vlib.us/beats/#plymell*

D.A. (David) Pratt "continues to continue" in a completely conventional community in Canada. He writes "poems that look like poems" – this is a phrase from Karl Ove Knausgaard's *My Struggle.*

Lauren Reynolds is a middle school English teacher and poet. She has two previously published chapbooks and a full-length collection. She has a master's degree in creative writing, with a concentration in poetry. Recurring themes include: memory, loss, coming of age and photography as an expression of the impermanence of time. She writes about the people she knows and imagines they might live, in the remnants of the once booming "car capital of the world", in Southeast Michigan. These are narratives of a world that has moved on, and those who struggle to make ends meet.

Kevin Ridgeway is the author of *Too Young to Know* (Stubborn Mule Press) and nine chapbooks of poetry including *Grandma Goes to Rehab* (Analog Submission Press, UK). His work can recently be found in *Slipstream, Chiron Review, Nerve Cowboy, Plainsongs, San Pedro River Review, The Cape Rock, Trailer Park Quarterly, Main Street Rag, Cultural Weekly* and *The American Journal of Poetry*, among others. He lives and writes in Long Beach, CA.

Brian Rihlmann was born in New Jersey and currently resides in Reno, Nevada. He writes free verse poetry, and has been published in The Blue Nib, The American Journal of Poetry, Cajun Mutt Press, The Rye Whiskey Review, and others. His first poetry collection, "Ordinary Trauma," (2019) was published by Alien Buddha Press.

Cindy Rinne creates fiber art and writes in San Bernardino, CA. She was Poet in Residence for the Neutra Institute Gallery and Museum, Los Angeles, CA. She has created fiber art for over 30 years, exhibiting internationally. Cindy collaborates in Performance Poetry using her own costume creations based on her books. A Pushcart nominee. Cindy is the author of several books: *Knife Me Split Memories* (Cholla Needles Press), *Letters Under Rock* with Bory Thach, (Elyssar Press), *Moon of Many Petals* (Cholla Needles Press), and others. Her poetry appeared or is forthcoming in: *Anti-Heroin Chic, Unpsychology Magazine, MORIA*, several anthologies, and others. *www.fiberverse.com*

Christopher Robin has written several books of poetry including: *Who Will Pay the Royalties for the Voices in My Head, Angelflies in My IdiotSoup* (Platonic3Way Press) and *Freaky Mumbler's Manifesto* (lulu.com). He spends his time between California, Oregon and Kansas, and calls no permanent place home. He is a flea market seller, cat-lover and dedicated vagabond.

He has 3 small books which are available at: *www.christopherrobinzenbaby.com* . He can be reached at: *junkwriter@christopherrobin.xyz*.

John D. Robinson is a UK poet: His poetry has appeared widely online and in print, establishing a strong presence within the small press: he has published several chapbooks and a handful of full collections: his latest publications are: 'The Sounds Of Samsara' (Cyberwit Publishing: India) 'Sharks & Butterflies' (Cajun Mutt Press: USA) and 'Red Dance' (Uncollected Press: USA): his first chapbook of short stories ' Smoking Herb & Other Stories' has just been published by Analog Submission Press: he was nominated for a 2019/2020 Pushcart Prize.

Judith Robinson is an editor, teacher, fiction writer, poet and visual artist. A 1980 summa cum laude graduate of the University of Pittsburgh, she is listed in the Directory of American Poets and Writers. She has published 75+ poems, five poetry collections, one fiction collection; one novel; edited or co-edited eleven poetry collections. Teacher: Osher at Carnegie Mellon University and the University of Pittsburgh. Her newest collection, "Carousel," was published in January, 2017, LUMMOX Press. Her last gallery exhibit "The Numbers Keep Changing," was on display at The Pittsburgh Holocaust Center, April -June, 2019. www.judithrrobinson.com alongtheserivers@gmail.com

Jean-Marie Romana is an accursed poet whose first poem was published when she was eight years old. She has a website at RomanaPoetry.com where she posts poems weekly. She lives in San Diego, California.

Dave Roskos is the editor of *Big Hammer* & *Street Value* magazines & Iniquity Press/Vendetta Books. He has recently been published in Alien Buddha, Concrete Mist Anthology, Fell Swoop, & Heroin Love Songs.

Covivitas

Congratulations to Lummox Press on

Lummox # 9

www.covivitas.com

Long Beach South Bay Area

R. Reza Handyman Services
Richard Reza, Supervisor

562.477.2590
borg2112@yahoo.com

Landscaping
Exterior/Interior Repairs
Painting
Plumbing
Electrical
Miscellaneous

Jen Dunford Roskos was born in Providence, RI and currently lives in Seaside Heights, NJ with her husband, poet and publisher Dave Roskos, a couple of cats, and a guinea pig. Her last book *Begging a Bowl of Birthrite Stew* was published by Iniquity Press/Vendetta Books in 2019.

C.C. Russell has published poetry, fiction, and non-fiction here and there across the web and in print. You can find his words in such places as Split Lip Magazine, Pidgeonholes, and the anthologies *Blood, Water, Wind, and Stone* and *Best Microfiction 2020*. He currently resides in Wyoming where he sometimes stares at the mountains when he should be writing. You can find more of his work at *ccrussell.net*

Patricia L. Scruggs is the author of *Forget the Moon*, a poetry collection. Her work has appeared in *ONTHEBUS, Spillway, RATTLE, Calyx, Cultural Weekly, Crab Creek Review, LUMMOX*, the anthologies *13 Los Angles Poets, So Luminous the Wildflowers*, and *Beyond the Lyric Moment*. A retired art educator, Patricia lives and writes in Southern California.

Arianna Sebo (she/her) is a queer poet and writer living in Southern Alberta with her husband, pug, and five cats. She works in the field of law to feed her family and writes poetry to feed her philosophical soul. Her poetry can be found in *Kissing Dynamite* and *45 Poems of Protest: The Pandemic* and is forthcoming in *Lucky Jefferson*. Follow her at *AriannaSebo.com* and *@AriannaSebo* on Twitter and Instagram.

Lisa Segal, an L.A. artist/poet/writer, uses typography, geometry, repetition, and hand-built multiples to continually reinvent a personal vocabulary of shapes and patterns. She's written three books—*Kicking Towards the Deep End* (poetry/prose); *Metamorphosis: Who is the Maker? An Artist's Statement* (her poetry, prose, and photographs of her sculptures); and *Trips* (a three-poet collection). Her textbook

Jack Grapes' Method Writing: The Brush Up is forthcoming in 2020. She's the 2017 L.A. Poet Society Poetry Month Contest winner and teaches poetry and writing through Los Angeles Poets & Writers. She's a founding member of StudioEleven, a Los Angeles art collective. *www.lisasegal.com*

Sanjeev Sethi is published in over 25 countries. He has more than 1200 poems printed or posted in venues around the world. Sethi's fourth poetry collection, *Wrappings in Bespoke*, is Winner of Full Fat Collection Competition-Deux organized by the Hedgehog Poetry Press (UK). It will be issued in 2020. He lives in Mumbai, India.

Renée M. Sgroi is an Associate Member of the League of Canadian Poets and the current President of the Brooklin Poetry Society in Brooklin (Ontario), Canada. Her work has appeared in Canadian journals such as *Synaeresis, The Prairie Journal*, and *The Banister*.

Eric Paul Shaffer is author of seven poetry volumes, including *Even Further West* (Winner of a 2019 Ka Palapala Poʻokela Book Award); *A Million-Dollar Bill; L?haina Noon; Portable Planet*; and *Living at the Monastery, Working in the Kitchen*. More than 500 poems appear in reviews in Australia, Canada, England, India, Iran, Ireland, Japan, the Netherlands, New Zealand, Nicaragua, Scotland, Wales, and the USA. Shaffer teaches composition, literature, and creative writing at Honolulu Community College.

Alima Sherman spends her time, raising children, living in a hundred-year-old house by the Pacific Ocean and taking care of her elderly chocolate lab. She is the author of *Above Houses, Broken Windows, Oceans*. Her poems have appeared in such journals as Nimrod, Poet Lore, Valparaiso, Poetry Review, Permafrost, and the Paterson Literary Review.

Nancy Shiffrin is the author of *THE VAST UNKNOWING* poems Infinity Publishing, B&N. com. She has other work available at lulu.com and from her personally at *nshiffrin@earthlink. net* . Last year she won the Angela Consolo Mankiewicz Poetry Prize.

Linda Singer writes poetry. Some people like her poetry. She likes those people. She co-hosts Poetry Apocalypse at the Angeles Gate Cultural Center in San Pedro every third Sunday. She does other things too. Come to the open mic at the Apocalypse and she'll tell you about them.

Judith Skillman is the recipient of awards from the Academy of American Poets and Artist Trust. She is the author of *The Truth about Our American Births*, Shanti Arts, 2020; and *Broken Lines—The Art & Craft of Poetry,* LUMMOX Press. Work has appeared in *Threepenny Review, Prairie Schooner, The Southern Review, Zyzzyva, We Refugees*, and other journals and anthologies. *www.judithskillman.com*

Rick Smith is a clinical psychologist specializing in brain damage and domestic violence; he practices in Rancho Cucamonga, Calif. He is a professional harmonica player who writes and plays for The Mescal Sheiks and can be heard on the soundtrack of the Academy Award Winning "Days of Heaven." Recent books are *The Wren Notebook* (2000); *Hard Landing* (2010) and *Whispering In A Mad Dog's Ear* (2014), all from LUMMOX Press. His essay "Snowed In With Carl Sandburg" appeared in the 2019 issue of Under The Sun. Check out his website: *docricksmith.com*

Donna Snyder founded the Tumblewords Project in 1995 and continues to organize its free weekly workshop series and other events in the El Paso borderlands. She has poetry collections published by Chimbarazu, Virgogray, and NeoPoiesis presses. Her poems, fiction, and reviews appear in such journals and anthologies as *Setu, Red Fez, Queen Mob's*

Teahouse, VEXT Magazine, Mezcla, Interstice, Original Resistance, and *Speak the Language of the Land.* Snyder has read her work in Alaska, California, Colorado, Massachusetts, New Mexico, New York, and Texas. She previously practiced law representing indigenous people, people with disabilities, and immigrant workers.

t. kilgore splake ("the cliffs dancer") lives in a tamarack location old mining row house in the ghost copper mining village of calumet in michigan's upper peninsula. as an artist splake has become a legend in the small press literary circles for his writing and photography. splake has several black-and-white photographs and poems in the new issue of "clutch" magazine, published by street corner presss in sister bay, wisconsin. his latest work is a chapbook manuscript that will use his photographs of the old railroad depot in calumet, michigan.

Jeanine Stevens is the author of *Limberlost* and *Inheritor* (Future Cycle Press). Her first poetry collection, Sailing on Milkweed was published by Cherry Grove Collections. Winner of the MacGuffin Poet Hunt, The Stockton Arts Commission Award, The Ekphrasis Prize and WOMR Cape Cod Community Radio National Poetry Award. *Brief Immensity*, won the Finishing Line Press Open Chapbook Award. Jeanine recently received her sixth Pushcart Nomination. She participated in Literary Lectures sponsored by Poets and Writers. Work has appeared in North Dakota Review, Pearl, Stoneboat, Rosebud, Chiron Review, and Forge. Jeanine studied poetry at U.C. Davis and California State University, Sacramento.

Lynn Tait is a poet/photographer living in Sarnia, Ontario Canada. Her poems have appeared in Vallum, FreeFall Literary Magazine, Literary Review of Canada, Contemporary Verse 2, and in over 100 North American anthologies including 7 LUMMOX anthologies

and Tamaracks by LUMMOX Press.
She is a member of The Ontario Poetry Society and the League Canadian Poets.

G. Murray Thomas moved from SoCal to upstate New York to care for his aging parents. Hence, these haiku and photos. You can follow his adventures and tribulations at *patreon.com/gmurraythomas*

H. Lamar Thomas lives in a glade of oak, elm and flowering maple, 25 acres of meadow and second growth hardwoods. It's a strange, beautiful oasis hidden between suburbs of noise and light. Slowly writing where once it was an avalanche of words a day, now forming journals of automatic writing and poems in darkness. The loner talking to trees and singing to his dog. 700 and counting publications, a rare [cook] book with LUMMOX Press, "A Romance with Food".

Bill Tremblay: poet, novelist, editor of *Colorado Review*, reviewer. He has books of poetry published, including *Crying in the Cheap Seats* [UMass Press], *Duhamel: Ideas of Order in Little Canada* [BOA Editions Ltd.], and *Shooting Script: Door of Fire* [EWU Press] which won the Colorado Book Award 2004 and *Walks Along the Ditch.* His novel, *The June Rise*, was given a star review on NPR's "All Things Considered" by Allan Cheuse. He has received fellowships from NEA, NEH, Fulbright Commission, as well as Pushcart Prize, *Best American Poetry*, and Yaddo. Bill founded the *Colorado Review* and served as its Editor for 15 years as it became a top 50 literary magazine in the US.

Maja Trochimczyk, Ph.D., is a Polish American poet, music historian, photographer, nonprofit director, and lightworker. The President of the California State Poetry Society, Managing Editor of the California Quarterly, President of Helena Modjeska Club, Board Secretary of the Polish American Historical Association,

Program Chair for Village Poets, and the Senior Director of Planning at Phoenix House California, she published 14 books of music history and poetry, and hundreds of poems, articles, and research studies in English, Polish and many translations. She manages Moonrise Press and seven blogs, with a commitment to compassionate, erudite service.

l. tyler-rickon is a writer and technical-theatre professional; their work explores the intersection of daily life, language, and the natural world we so readily forget we are part of. They live with their loving and supportive spouse not far from Griffith Park and the Glendale Narrows in Los Angeles, and love their neighbors: hawks, black-necked stilts, cormorants, and coyotes. You may find more of their work in the 2020 edition of the Altadena Literary Review.

Katharine VanDewark finds the truncation of words: "veggies," "EVOO," "ADD," to name only a few, annoying. However, "WTF" is useful either spoken or written. "OMG" only works on the page. And who remembers how to spell deoxyribonucleic acid without looking it up??

Richard Vidan was discharged from the Army as "unsuitable for military service." Briefly a petty/mid-level, non-violent criminal. Writer/actor with the avant-garde critically-acclaimed Storefront Theatre. Volunteer head cook/resident atheist for 13 years on Thursdays at a church soup kitchen. Poet and Outsider Artist for 45+ years. Married to infamous blues singer Zola Moon, which he likens to being in a flaming hurricane. Remains angry about almost everything. Excellent shot with a variety of firearms. Favorite food: the flesh of the rich. Hobbies: motorcycles, billiards, poker, arson, amateur brain surgery. Motto: Vivez comme si vous étiez déjà mort (Live as if you are already dead).

Lawrence Welsh has published 12 books of poetry, including *Begging for Vultures: New* *and Selected Poems* (University of New Mexico Press). His books have won the Southwest Book Award, the New Mexico-Arizona Book Award, the Southwest Books of the Year Award and have been short listed for the PEN Southwest Book Award and the Writers' League of Texas Book Award. His poetry, reviews, essays, as well as journalistic writings, have appeared in more than 300 national and regional magazines, journals, newspapers and anthologies.

Charles Wilkinson's work includes *The Pain Tree and Other Stories* (London Magazine Editions). His poems have been in *Poetry Wales, Poetry Salzburg* (Austria), *Shearsman, New Walk, Magma, Under the Radar, Tears in the Fence, Scintilla, Envoi, Stand, Snow lit rev* and other journals. A pamphlet, *Ag & Au,* came out from Flarestack Poets in 2013. His full-length poetry collection, *The Glazier's Choice*, appeared from Eyewear in 2019; it has been nominated for a Forward Prize. He lives in Powys, Wales, where he is heavily outnumbered by members of the ovine community. More information about his work can be found at his website: *http://charleswilkinonauthor.com*

Lyn White lives in north Wales. Her work is influenced by issues of social justice and events, places and people she has known or imagined. She is especially interested in exploring the boundaries of dream, fantasy and reality. Her poem *'A Rose For Gaza'* was shortlisted for the *Theatre Cloud 'War Poetry for Today' competition 2014.* This and many other poems, have been widely published on line and in print.

Pamela Williams is a poet and artist also offering content writing and editing, with a fine art/design background, and a lifelong habit of artistic expression. Her grounded heartland upbringing provided the springboard for thirty expansive years in the San Francisco area, where the vibrant culture, spectacular geography, and her antique business offered a parade of provocative fodder for her writing. New Mexico's extreme contrasts and rich history are now fueling alchemical inspiration through its proffered seductions and mysterious remnants of multi-cultural heritage, feeding her current writing/assemblage work and her first collection of poetry, 'Hair on Fire', available at amazon. com: *http://amzn.to/2eD5lxL*. Her writing is most recently driven by the loss of her husband, inspiring diving more deeply into the miracles of this journey.

A Pushcart Prize and Best of the Net nominee, **Kelsey Bryan-Zwick** is a Spanish/English speaking poet from Long Beach, California. Disabled with scoliosis from a young age, her poems often focus on trauma, giving heart to the antiseptic language of hospital intake forms. Author of *Watermarked* (Sadie Girl Press) and founder of the micro-press BindYourOwnBooks, Kelsey's poems have been accepted by *Spillway, Trailer Park Quarterly, Cholla Needles, Rise Up Review, Right Hand Pointing, Redshift,* and *Making Up*, a Picture Show Press anthology. Writing towards her new title, *Here Go the Knives*, find her at *www.kelseybryanzwick.wixsite. com/poetry*.

Raindog

SEE YOU ALL
AROUND
CAMPUS

NUMBER NINE
2020

Made in the USA
Middletown, DE
15 September 2020

19919164R20124